Feeding on God's Word

SUSAN SAYERS

kevin mayhew

First published in 2002 by KEVIN MAYHEW LTD
Buxhall, Stowmarket, Suffolk IP14 3BW
Email: info@kevinmayhewltd.com

These texts first appeared in *Living Stones – Complete
Resource Book, Year B*

9 8 7 6 5 4 3 2 1 0

ISBN 1 84003 934 5
Catalogue No 1500522

Cover design by Jonathan Stroulger
Edited by Katherine Laidler

Printed and bound in Great Britain

Foreword

These reflections on the weekly readings are not new material – they come from the Complete Resource Book in the *Living Stones* programme, which follows the Common Worship Lectionary in the Anglican Church. Their publication in this separate book – here covering the readings for Year B – has been widely requested from various sources and for various reasons.

- Those who cannot get to church often, or who receive communion at home or in hospital, would like some help with reading the weekly Bible passages so they can be spiritually fed, and feel more part of the ongoing exploration of Scripture by the rest of the congregation.

- Discussion groups deciding to focus on the following week's readings express a need for the collected reflections in a separate book so that each group member can have a copy.

- Individuals wanting to prepare themselves for the worship Sunday by Sunday, or reflect on the previous week's readings, would like a book to help them. *Feeding on God's Word* serves this need.

- Those leading intercessions and reading the Bible passages during worship would value the reflections to help in their preparation.

- Those planning work with children and young people would like each team member to have a copy of the Scripture references and the reflection on those readings in order to feed them spiritually and better inform their prayer and preparation. Their own insights can then be incorporated in their ministry.

- Those with the talk or sermon to prepare would like their own copy of the Bible references and reflections to jump-start sermon preparation.

So, having heard all the requests, here is the book! I hope it will be useful to you all. These reflections don't pretend to be anything more than my own thinking as I read and pray the Scripture passages for each week. But I do believe that as more and more people in the church commit themselves to praying for God's guiding, reading the Bible sections for each Sunday, and reflecting on them with the help of a book like this, together with a good commentary where necessary, the whole people of God will be fed – properly fed in a deep and wholesome way.

We are called to be bread-sharers as Christians, and that includes both word and sacrament. As we share the meal of Scripture week by week, as well as the meal of bread and wine, we will be nourished and strengthened for the daily work of love to which God invites us.

SUSAN SAYERS

Contents

First Sunday of Advent

Thought for the day
Be alert and watchful; keep yourselves ready.

Reflection on the readings
Isaiah 64:1-9; Psalm 80:1-7, 17-19
1 Corinthians 1:3-9; Mark 13:24-37

There is a sense, in the reading from Isaiah, that, but for God's mercy, we are in a hopeless situation. Even as we beg for God's help, recognising that he has proved himself to be the one and only real God, we know that our behaviour has been a rejection of all God is and values. So what point can there be in asking for help from the One we spend so much time ignoring, rejecting and dismissing?

Yet there is hope; the prophet clings on to the fact that we are of God's making. Perhaps his love and affection for us will, even now, move God to show mercy to his wayward creation of humankind. Psalm 80 echoes this pleading for rescue and restoration, undeserved as it is. Both these readings from the Old Testament give us a flavour of the generations of longing and yearning for a saviour, often from the pit of human experience and in a very candid recognition of the human condition.

In contrast, the reading from Paul's letter to the Christians in Corinth is written after the coming of Jesus, the promised Saviour. It is full of the confidence which comes from knowing that, though we cannot save ourselves and our weaknesses are as weak as ever, the life of Jesus in us has power to keep us strong to the end and uphold us in what is right and good. God has indeed acted with an outpouring of unearned and undeserved love and generosity, simply because it is

God's nature to act with grace and mercy. Since God is utterly faithful, we can trust him even with the worst of ourselves; his power in us is always going to be sufficient.

Today's Gospel is Jesus speaking to us of real and serious things. Never does Jesus pretend to us; never does he gloss over costs or dangers. Treating us with respect, he warns us so as to prepare us, and we need to take notice of what he is saying. He is speaking of great cosmic turmoil, and disturbing self-appointed leaders with power to attract and lead many astray. We are warned against gullibility and fashion-chasing where truth is concerned. Even Jesus is not in possession of the exact times and dates, but he is concerned to pass on to his followers, with considerable urgency, the need to be alert and watchful, so that whatever time the end comes we will be ready and prepared.

Second Sunday of Advent

Thought for the day

John the Baptist prepares the way for the coming of the
Messiah by helping the people to realign their lives.

Reflection on the readings

Isaiah 40:1-11; Psalm 85:1-2, 8-13
2 Peter 3:8-15a; Mark 1:1-8

Mark's Gospel bursts straight in with the dynamic claim
that we are hearing about nothing less than the Messiah, the
Son of God, entering into the realm of ordinary human life.
Just as the prophet Isaiah had foretold, this event would
require some drastic preparation work, and here is John (we
are given no other introductory details about him) suddenly fulfilling the old prophecy and urging people to get
their lives and attitudes sorted out and cleaned up. He is
using the effective symbolism of baptismal washing as a
sign of washed lives. If you are willing to step into the river,
publicly, confess your sins and be pushed down under the
water as a sign of your repentance, you are quite likely to
mean what you say, and emerge from the experience full of
new, fresh enthusiasm for walking God's way.

This is exactly the thorough kind of repentance we all
need regularly. Perhaps we should use every shower and
bath time as an opportunity for such spiritual washing.
Then we would experience daily the fresh start and open-
ness provided by God's forgiveness of acknowledged and
confessed sin.

Along with John's call to thorough repentance and baptismal washing was the message he preached, directing his
followers to look for the powerful person of great honour

who would be coming shortly and whose baptism would be not with water but the Holy Spirit of God. Just imagine standing dripping and cleansed by the Jordan as you hear about someone who will drench and immerse you in the holiness of the Spirit of God. It must have triggered in many the deep longing and expectant thirsting for God which allows lives to be shaken, hearts to be softened and the kingdom to come.

The same is true now. It is as an expectant people, thirsty for God and longing for a total immersing in his life, that we prepare during the season of Advent for the festival of Christmas. The extent to which we respond to John's call across the centuries will determine how open and receptive we are to welcoming Jesus and allowing him into our lives. The life which Peter describes – of harmony, repaying even evil with blessing, and doing good regardless of the conse- quences – is a direct result of living immersed in the Holy Spirit of God.

Third Sunday of Advent

Thought for the day

In Jesus, God will be fulfilling the Messianic prophecies about the promised Saviour.

Reflection on the readings

Isaiah 61:1-4, 8-11; Psalm 126 or Canticle: Magnificat
1 Thessalonians 5:16-24; John 1:6-8, 19-28

Advent almost engulfs us with its spirit of urgent preparation. Everyone writes lists and tries to organise food, apt presents and thematic decorations; the store cupboard fills with things no one is allowed to touch yet, and tops of wardrobes become hiding places for bulky secrets. The Church's season of Advent is a kind of spiritual equivalent of all this, not just because we are rehearsing Christmas carols and Nativity plays, but because we are standing alongside the people of Israel in their period of waiting and preparation for the coming of the promised Saviour. In these four weeks we can sense something of their generations of waiting and longing.

It is the Messiah's Advent that we journey through at this time of year, and here too we find checklists and plans, secrets and mysteries, half-seen puzzles, and truths which have yet to be unpacked and savoured. The Isaiah reading for today is a case in point. We are given a kind of checklist of pointers to look out for in the promised Saviour, which will ensure that we recognise him when he comes. It is a wonderful checklist, full of hope and freshness, the overturning of negatives and the victory of good over evil.

Hearing either Psalm 126 or the Magnificat from the standpoint of the Isaiah passage is like having a peep into the wrapped future, and sensing that on Christmas morning we shall not be disappointed. And, of course, the Incarnation of Christmas morning is indeed the unwrapping of that promised secret. Even as John the Baptist was teaching by the River Jordan, he knew that the Christ was already there among them, though still hidden, since his public ministry had not yet begun. It would not be long before those qualities on Isaiah's list could be checked out and validated by the people, provided they had eyes open to recognise in Jesus all that the prophets had foretold.

But at the moment we are still in the waiting place, and all that is in the future. For now, we sense the expectancy of the faithful people of Israel, and also recognise our own place of waiting for that final coming of total accomplishment at the end of time. We live with our hopes and our questions, our puzzles and our trust in the faithful God. We know that in God's way all the checklists of qualities and characteristics both for the first and the second coming will hold good.

John the Baptist finds the authorities trying to do a full story on him, mistakenly homing in on the messenger instead of the coming King. He describes himself, in the words of the prophet, as simply a voice – not to be curiously interviewed, but heard, with the heart as well as the ears. We can make this Advent such a time of listening to the real message, rather than being sidetracked by all the less important things. The reading from Thessalonians gives us sound, practical ideas for this.

Fourth Sunday of Advent

Thought for the day

God's promised kingdom, announced both to King David
in ancient times and to Mary by the angel Gabriel,
will go on for ever.

Reflection on the readings

2 Samuel 7:1-11, 16
Canticle: Magnificat or Psalm 89:1-4, 19-26
Romans 16:25-27; Luke 1:26-38

When King David is filled with enthusiasm for building a
great and holy temple to house the ark of the covenant, his
offer is turned down, but the graciousness of his attitude
very much accepted by God. Through the prophet Nathan,
God points out to David that the seeming permanence of a
grand building is nothing to be compared with the real
permanence of the eternally present God. With such a
nature there is no problem with flexibility; eternal Presence
can move wherever the people go, untied by structural
foundations.

Having assured King David that the building idea will
be taken up by his son, God reveals his own blueprint for
an everlasting kingdom, and the coming of a reign within
the royal House of David which will eventually spread
throughout the whole world. It was out of this promise
that the hope of God's Messiah was born, particularly in
the dark years following the collapse of the monarchy.
Gradually the understanding of this Messiah became less
tied in people's minds with temporal ruling power and
more with a priestly kind of kingship which would bring
worldwide blessing and hope.

So when we find Gabriel visiting Mary with a message that her son will reign on the throne of his ancestor, David, and his kingdom will never end, we are listening in on a gathering together of all the hopes and longings of generations, right back to King David himself. By this time, the overtones of a Messianic, priestly kingship will be there, and through Mary those hopes and plans can be accomplished for the saving of the whole world.

The passage from Romans gives us a glorious sense of a crescendo as the full spread of God's kingdom builds to completion. John Ellerton's well-loved hymn *The day thou gavest, Lord, is ended* puts it like this:

> So be it, Lord; thy throne shall never,
> like earth's proud empires, pass away;
> thy kingdom stands and grows for ever
> till all thy creatures own thy sway.

Our amazing privilege is to be part of the building.

Christmas Day

Thought for the day
Jesus Christ, the world's Saviour, is here with us,
born as a human baby.

Reflection on the readings
Isaiah 62:6-12; Psalm 97
Titus 3:4-7; Luke 2:(1-7) 8-20

Dogs and cats will never let you forget that it's feeding time. They go on and on reminding you loudly until you do something about that empty bowl. At the same time they are voicing (and wagging) their excitement that you will definitely be feeding them because you always do. Today's reading from the book of Isaiah has a lovely sense of God's watchmen being posted where they can see what is going on, and given clear instructions to keep shouting both their need for God to send the promised Saviour, and their faith that he will, until he acts. Christmas is the great celebration of that action – of God breaking into his creation in a new and extraordinary way in order to save us.

Like the shepherds, we have been getting on with our daily and nightly lives, and on this night we remember the splash of God's glory across the sky, and the cry of a newborn child on a heap of straw. The ordinary and the extraordinary are shaken together, the hopes and promises become fused in practical reality, and the whole world is closer to salvation than ever before.

The Incarnation – with all its risk, its glory laid aside, its daring love – speaks as clearly to us, two thousand years on, as it did to those shepherds marvelling at the angels' message as they discovered the baby in the stable. Marvelling is filled with questions as well as wonder, and most of us find that God's presence in our world as a human baby raises many questions. Such questions are to be valued, as they can lead us forward into deeper understanding.

We are told that Mary kept all these questions and pondered them in her heart. Christmas is a time for such pondering, as well as the more usual feasting and celebrating. Wrapped up in those swaddling bands is God's answer to our longing for inner peace, our need for healing and wholeness, and our recognition that we cannot save ourselves no matter what effort we put into it. The baby in Mary's arms is God hearing our hidden fears and tears, and coming in person to save us and set us free.

First Sunday of Christmas

Thought for the day

Just as the angels said, a Saviour has been born for us.

Reflection on the readings

Isaiah 61:10-62:3; Psalm 148
Galatians 4:4-7; Luke 2:15-21

Right from the very beginning of his life on earth Jesus is revolutionary in his mission. Born as the bringer of God's saving power and justice, Mary gives birth to him on the straw of a stable, far from home and family support. Those who came hot-footing it along the streets in the middle of the night to welcome him were neither familiar neighbours nor religious leaders but shepherds, who were considered unclean and unrighteous due to the nature of their job. Yet it was to them that Luke reports the angels coming, a sign that this Saviour is linked both with David the shepherd boy turned king, and also the marginalised and the powerless. It is not dutiful legalism affirmed here, but the grace of God's wide, unconditional love.

Christmas is often known as the season of goodwill, taken up from the angels' message, and many push the boat out at Christmas in trying to live as people of goodwill, at least over the bank holiday! Sadly the effort and the expectations of goodwill-living are a great strain, with the result that Christmas is also the season when fragile relationships in families explode or implode, and suicide rates are higher than usual. Duty is a terrible burden and weighs our living down.

That's why this baby we welcome into the world at Christmas is such good news. There is a shift of emphasis away from the hopeless struggle most of us know of honestly living up to what we feel we are supposed to be: the heavy duty route. In contrast, this child is already spreading different news, which really is good to hear. Our calling is simply to be ourselves, human beings with a particular, unique set of genes, in the image and likeness of the God who created us.

This means that the more we allow ourselves to be the unmerited recipients of God's giving, and stop trying to impress him, ourselves and one another with what we are not, the more our real selves we will become, and the more Godlike we shall grow in the process. That is occasion for cosmic rejoicing!

Second Sunday of Christmas

Thought for the day

The Word made flesh at Christmas was always with God,
always expressing his creative love.

Reflection on the readings

Jeremiah 31:7-14 or Ecclesiasticus 24:1-12
Psalm 147:12-20 or
Canticle: Wisdom of Solomon 10:15-21
Ephesians 1:3-14
John 1:(1-9) 10-18

Sympathy cards will often bear messages like 'A word of comfort . . .', and the whole idea of sending cards of sympathy to those who are distressed or grieving is the knowledge that the expressed sympathy of another human, sharing the anguish, can be so supportive and comforting.

The supreme Word of comfort and hope to all of us in any age and every circumstance is the Word of God's loving wisdom, lying here among us as a human baby in the hay. All the nakedness, vulnerability and self-giving, which assure us of real, trustworthy love, are here, spelt out to us in the Christmas season as we marvel at the intimacy of God with his people, the Creator with the created.

All through the process of creation, this expressive Word of love has drawn life and hope into tangible form. All through the developing discernment of spiritual things, the expressive Word has spoken eternal truth and mystery, Godliness and the way of love.

So Christmas does not spring on to our consciousness a raw, untried and untested phenomenon, out of nowhere. The Incarnation tenderly affirms and shows in person all that the human spirit had sensed through the ages, and the created world from the first calling of light into darkness and order into chaos.

The Epiphany

Thought for the day

Jesus, the promised Messiah,
is shown to the Gentile world.

Reflection on the readings

Isaiah 60:1-6; Psalm 72:(1-9) 10-15
Ephesians 3:1-12; Matthew 2:1-12

We are well used to thinking of the Church's call as out-reach. Partly this is because of the empty chairs we have got used to seeing around us each Sunday and on week-days. Partly it is a growing awareness of the deep spiritual hunger of many who have not been brought up to go to church and do not see it as a viable answer to their need. So there is almost a daydream quality for us, as well as the dispirited people of Israel, when we are asked to imagine crowds and crowds of people from all walks of life, actively seeking us out, in order to find God and spiritual fulfilment.

I wonder how the Church would cope with such a situation? Would we be able to help them with their search? Would we understand their questions? Would we be over-joyed to see them pouring through the doors, or would they pose a threat to our traditional way of doing things?

When we recognise that being 'a light to lighten the Gentiles' can actually be quite disturbing, we can start to understand something of the hesitation the Jewish people had about welcoming the early Christians, many of them totally 'unsynagogued'. We can also thrill to the hope of a new direction – of a Church on the grow at last. The signs are there, and the tide is turning.

Epiphany has therefore particular significance for us at the moment. The light of the world is for everyone – all groups and nations, all cultures and ages, not just those we are familiar with or approve of, or who know 'how we do it' in our own church. Since most of us are Gentiles ourselves, the significance of Christ being shown to the Gentile 'outsiders' tends to pass us by unnoticed, unless we ask ourselves another question. Which 'outsiders' might those wise men represent today? To enter into the spirit of Epiphany we need to alter our vision until we understand that God has no outsiders, and no person or group is excluded. It was God's delight to reveal his baby Son to searching pagan foreigners.

As we hear once again the story of these outsiders, travelling many miles over difficult terrain in order to find for themselves the world's enlightenment, we could do well to bear in mind all those in our own times who are spiritually awake and searching, many travelling over difficult terrain, and make sure that we light the lamps, ready to welcome them.

The Baptism of Christ:
First Sunday of Epiphany

Thought for the day

Through the Holy Spirit, Jesus is affirmed at his
Baptism as God's beloved Son, and we too are given
the Spirit of God which affirms us as God's
adopted daughters and sons.

Reflection on the readings

Genesis 1:1-5; Psalm 29
Acts 19:1-7; Mark 1:4-11

The believers Paul found at Ephesus had never heard of the
Holy Spirit. They had made the decision to repent of their
sins and change the way they lived, but had not realised that
God's Spirit could actually live in them to make this change
a reality. There are still many people today who value Jesus'
ethical teaching, and use his guidelines as ideals to strive for,
but have not taken on board as a real possibility that God's
life can live in them, changing them from the inside out.

We have to acknowledge that it is indeed an odd concept.
All the time we are making decisions of the will – about
which potatoes to buy for baking, which make of car to go
for, whether to stop smoking or carry on, whether to give
money to an appeal or not. We also make decisions about
life direction – we decide to marry, or to complete the tax
return honestly, to campaign for justice or to eat no meat.
All this reinforces that we are in control of our own lives, as
mature, independent people.

The Holy Spirit can sound like a takeover bid, and many
are suspicious of this, and find it all rather far-fetched. Yes,

we can choose to live God's way, as rational human beings, but aren't we kidding ourselves to talk about God's life and Spirit actually taking up residence?

All today's readings give us evidence of the real living Spirit of God at work. The Spirit broods over the chaos and breathes God's creative life into it. As Jesus is baptised God's Spirit settles on him, affirming his identity and his mission. And in Acts we hear how a random group of representative new Christians breaks into a whole new dimension of living faith as they are baptised with both water and the Holy Spirit. God breaks into our human confines with his divine nature, and that opens up possibilities of full life which could never otherwise happen. Rather than a takeover bid, it is a setting free; rather than kidding ourselves, it is truth in all its fullness.

Second Sunday of Epiphany

Thought for the day
Jesus, the Christ, unlocks the mysteries of God.

Reflection on the readings
1 Samuel 3:1-10 (11-20); Psalm 139:1-6, 13-18
Revelation 5:1-10; John 1:43-51

Generally it makes us uncomfortable if someone claims to be able to 'read us like a book'. Are we that simplistic? Is there no unique mystery about us which is hardly fathomable to ourselves, let alone another person? If we know this to be true for individual human mysteries, how much more so is it true of God. None of us, and no particular group, can realistically claim to 'know' God fully and discern his nature; we are simply provided with a lifetime each, to travel a little deeper into the mystery that is God.

The season of Epiphany is all about God being revealed, and it is to the young child, Samuel, that God reveals something of his thoughts; to one who is still innocent of life's ethical complications which so often cloud our spiritual vision as adults. Samuel becomes an intermediary between God and Eli, whose short sight is not only physical.

Psalm 139 celebrates the intimate knowing which God has of us, having been totally involved with us from conception to birth and beyond. Simply the thought of God knowing us so well is something the psalmist finds mind-blowing, since it emphasises the extensiveness of God which surpasses all we can imagine.

In the reading from Revelation we have that terrible picture of all God's thoughts locked up for ever, since no one can be found who is worthy to break the seals on the scroll. John weeps at the hopelessness of it, until the figure of the Christ appears who has become human, has given up his life and triumphed through love, so that the secrets of God can be revealed through him.

We need to grasp the urgency and immediacy of this vision, and the life of Jesus in the Gospels. Do we, as we plead for the world and its people, weep for the places where God is not being made known, and weep for the souls to whom the truth of God's love is not being revealed? We, who are privileged to have met with Jesus, are the only ones who can spread news of who the true God is, as revealed in Jesus Christ. We are the ones in this generation who can speak it in language our contemporaries understand. And if we don't, the thoughts of God, which the world desperately needs, will remain effectively closed and inaccessible.

Third Sunday of Epiphany

Thought for the day

Signs of glory lead us to believe in Jesus as Lord
and Saviour.

Reflection on the readings

Genesis 14:17-20; Psalm 128
Revelation 19:6-10; John 2:1-11

Melchizedek is a strange, shadowy figure, who emerges
briefly in the Book of Genesis as an ancient priest-king
bearing gifts of bread and wine and a blessing from the
great God of heaven for Abram. He is almost more sign
than character, a bringer of God's gifts and perhaps the
reassurance of God's blessing which Abram badly needed
at the time. God will use all kinds of unexpected people
and situations to speak his love to us, often just when we
most need to be reassured of it.

The changing of water into wine at the wedding party in
Cana is described by John as being a sign of glory in Jesus,
which led his disciples to believe in him. This, too, is a
strange, mysterious sign, quite unlike many of the other
Gospel stories. It is recorded as being the first of the signs
Jesus did, and takes place immediately after the disciples are
called. Since Mary is aware of the wine shortage she is presumably a close friend or relative of the family, and she is
convinced that her Son will be able to help them out of a difficult situation. But unlike many other Gospel events, this
isn't a healing, it isn't a matter of great importance, and the
family hasn't asked Jesus for help. The water is not spoken
to (as in the calming of the waves) and the disciples are not
being asked to act in faith but are merely onlookers.

Certainly the servants show great faith in serving water as wine to the chief guest; the tone of Mary's instructions had obviously convinced them that it would be worth their while doing exactly what the young man said, no matter how odd it sounded. Mary herself is a sign in this episode, directing the servants, and all of us, to 'do whatever he tells you'. But we are left wondering why Jesus' power was used in this 'parochial' way at this stage in his ministry at Mary's insistent request, and whether the chief guest was ever allowed into the secret so he, too, could marvel. What is clear is that Jesus Christ is named here as having authority over the created world. Water into wine is a natural process, but a long one in terms of time. In this miracle, we glimpse life in terms of eternity, rather than being trapped in time. We and the disciples are led to see Jesus himself in terms of eternity and authority.

The reading from Revelation reinforces this, as with John we hear the great thunder of voices lifted in praise and worship, honouring the one in whom the victory of goodness and truth is accomplished for ever. However tempted we are to give worship to the bearers of God's good news, we are reminded here that all worship is to be directed only to the true and living God.

Fourth Sunday of Epiphany

Thought for the day

Jesus displays all the signs that mark him out
to be God's chosen One.

Reflection on the readings

Deuteronomy 18:15-20; Psalm 111
Revelation 12:1-5a; Mark 1:21-28

When Moses had approached God on the holy mountain, the people had watched all the signs of God's power and mystery and been so terrified of such a close encounter with the almighty One that they had trembled and begged Moses to act as intermediary for them. God's holiness threw their sinfulness into terrible focus and they knew they couldn't cope with such purity.

We find a similar reaction in today's Gospel, when a man in the congregation breaks the awed hush following Jesus' teaching, to scream out in the quiet synagogue. We can imagine the panic and horror expressed in that uncontrolled outburst. What could have set it off? Was the man merely a familiar local madman, used to disrupting the orderly services?

Mark suggests that this was something startlingly different from a mad heckler. Something has thrown the man into a frenzy of fear, and it seems to be linked with the way Jesus has been behaving. So what has Jesus been doing? We are told he has been teaching, and his teaching, unlike the usual preachers, has the distinct ring of authority.

Presumably so much of God's glory shone through Jesus' words and manner that it was highly challenging, and therefore offensive, to whatever in the man was evil, and in opposition to God's nature. He could not face the light of God's goodness shining into his soul and showing it up for what it really was. That carried with it a sense of horror at the destruction bound to come to that evil, if God were to get too close. So he screams out, seeing the loving God only in terms of cauterising purity.

And in one sense the man was right. Whatever we are – both the evil and the good – cannot be hidden from God, and as we allow him close, the evil cannot survive the power of his love. In Jesus, God's transcendent glory becomes immanent, in the only way this can happen without our destruction: in the complete self-giving of the cross.

Proper 1

Thought for the day

The good news about God is far too good
to keep to ourselves.

Reflection on the readings

Isaiah 40:12-31; Psalm 147:1-11, 20c
1 Corinthians 9:16-23; Mark 1:29-39

In the Isaiah reading for today we find a valiant effort to get us thinking, and imagining the unimaginable. The prophet is trying to help us glimpse something of the vast and limitless essence of the Being we know as God, whose creation we inhabit. We are taken on a quick guided tour of the universe, marvelling at the God who made it all and whose creative loving holds it all and sustains it. From time to time the prophet gives up on the descriptions as totally inadequate for the amazing reality, and simply points out how crazy it is even to attempt any comparisons with the living God. The wonder of God beats everything, and leaves us open-mouthed and speechless when we get any-where near the truth of his nature.

The Psalm echoes these thoughts, and then we find Paul, in his letter to the Christians in Corinth, so excited at spreading the good news about God that he is quite happy to devote his whole life and energy to it. There is utter dedication to the cause in the way he does his research and fits his language and teaching programme to the diverse needs and backgrounds of his hearers.

Why is he so willing to adapt himself and put himself out? Because his encounter with the living God has revolu-tionised his own life; the God he has met personally through

Jesus is simply so wonderful that he can't bear anyone to get through the rest of their life without knowing about him.

In today's Gospel we hear about Jesus' enthusiasm for spreading the good news. He has set Peter's mother-in-law free of her fever, and liberated all kinds of other visitors to the house from their mental, physical and spiritual suffering. We know that following this concentration of healing ministry, Jesus rises before it's light, in order to spend time in prayer, and when his friends find him, wanting to take him back to the community who are asking for him, he is instead concerned to move on. Having seen the look of liberation in the eyes of those set free in Capernaum, he cannot wait to spread the good news of God's freeing love far and wide.

It is whenever we get a fresh and breathtaking experience of who God is and what he is like, that we find ourselves longing for others to share what we have discovered, and cannot wait to pass the good news on.

Proper 2

Thought for the day

Jesus wants to heal us to wholeness,
and to him no one is untouchable.

Reflection on the readings

2 Kings 5:1-14; Psalm 30
1 Corinthians 9:24-27; Mark 1:40-45

To be considered untouchable is a terrible thing. To have
people shrink away from you, either openly or more subtly,
and to watch them draw their children out of your contamin-
ating danger, inflicts deep wounds on the psyche, almost
worse than the illness itself. It is not only leprosy; AIDS
sufferers can meet the same kind of rejection, the Dalits of
India are stamped with it from birth, and political regimes
can concoct it legally and devastatingly, as, for example, in
Apartheid. Any who live under tyranny and oppression,
whether in police states or in dysfunctional family homes,
are familiar with the erosive wearing-down of it. To some
extent all minorities experience it, and only those who have
been on the receiving end can have any idea of the effect it
has on self-esteem and the capacity to relate positively with
others.

Our readings today show us God's attitude to untouchability in all its forms. We read of Naaman's wife's servant
girl from Israel, who instinctively knows that God would
like to restore her master to wholeness. Through Elisha the
prophet, Naaman is offered God's healing. It is decep-
tively simple, being based on humility and obedience,

both of which are bound to cause an angry reaction in a highly respected, wealthy army commander. As far as God is concerned, Naaman is no special case because of his position or wealth; he is a special case because he is a child of God, created and loved into being, as are we all. That is what makes God eager to bring people to wholeness, whoever they are.

In the Gospel we meet another leper, in whom the years of untouchability have taken their toll. He can hardly believe that anyone would want to be bothered with him. He has come to see himself as others have treated him. Yet he senses that with Jesus there may be a spark of hope and, illegally, the man approaches him, doubting not his power but his desire to help. And how does Jesus react?

With anger. This comes as a shock, and some manuscripts have Jesus being moved with compassion, which is perhaps more what we might expect. But it is worth looking at the stern, strong words Jesus uses in reply. Emphatically he insists that of course he wants to heal the man. It may well be that he wants things done properly in keeping with the law, and that is why he directs the man to do what the law requires, going to show himself to the priest. But surely the overriding impression we are left with is of Jesus willingly touching what is considered untouchable, and making him whole, not only physically but holistically.

If this is God's nature, then it also needs to be ours. We cannot claim to be followers of Christ and live comfortably with any kind of marginalising, or any system which makes human beings out to be untouchable for any reason. If untouchability makes us angry, and urges us to do what we can to bring about change, then we shall be offering the touch of our healing God.

Proper 3

Sunday between 17 and 23 February inclusive
(if earlier than the Second Sunday before Lent)

Thought for the day

The Son of Man has authority on earth to forgive sins.

Reflection on the readings

Isaiah 43:18-25; Psalm 41
2 Corinthians 1:18-22; Mark 2:1-12

Most of us have at some point in life got stuck in a guilt zone. Whatever it was that we did or failed to do keeps washing around in our head and refuses to disappear. It alters our outlook and our attitude to the present, it distorts our capacity for walking freely into the future, and can, if we let it, actually drive us further into guilt-ridden places! The prophet speaking in today's passage from Isaiah obviously understands what it feels like to be trapped by guilt about the past. And so, of course, does the God who made us.

The passage is like a breath of fresh air: God is saying to us that we can stop thinking about all those past things, and put them behind us once and for all, because he is about to do something completely new. It is described in images of hope taken from the natural world – water in the wilderness and rivers in the desert. And why is God embarking on such a comprehensive forgiveness programme, erasing the guilt of the past in this way?

It is not because of anything his people have done to earn it, but simply because it is God's very nature to set people free like this. Since he is God he can't help doing it! And it is therefore not surprising that we find Jesus exercising authority over sin in the same way. The scribes, knowing their scripture, are quite right in observing that only God can forgive sins. They know that he alone has the authority over evil to erase it and render it powerless, thereby setting people free of its effects in the rest of their lives.

So when Jesus picks up on their thoughts and asks whether they think it is harder to forgive sins or make a paralysed body mobile again, he is leading them to the point where they will have proof of Jesus' identity. They are about to see, in the outward body, what only God is able to do in the realm of the human spirit. Just as the forgiveness has unlocked and liberated the man's spirit, so now his limbs are unlocked, setting him free also physically. Surely the authenticity of the one will convince them of the authenticity of the other? Only if they have eyes open to see.

In the passage from 2 Corinthians, Paul spells out the great truth which the scribes could not cope with: that all the promises of God have their 'Yes' in Christ. The liberating power of God's forgiveness is physically shown in the person of Jesus, and its vitalising effects continue to liberate prisoners two thousand years on.

Second Sunday before Lent

Thought for the day
Christ is the image of the unseen God.

Reflection on the readings
Proverbs 8:1, 22-31; Psalm 104:24-35
Colossians 1:15-20; John 1:1-14

Last week we were reflecting on the forgiving nature of God, and today, with the reading from Proverbs to help us, it is as if we are savouring the extraordinary creative energy of God's wisdom, holding it and marvelling at it, personalised for accessibility. What is God's wisdom like? With a poet's vision it is described as a creative woman, sensitive, delighting in all the unfolding wonders, appreciating and valuing with a childlike innocence which is playful, yet candid and pure.

It is a lovely if unexpected image, and helps us to understand more of God's nature. There is a lightness and gentleness of touch here which acts as a balance to our more usual serious-minded image of a God of power and responsibility. We sense a wonderful harmony of what we, from our separate-gendered perspective, might see as the masculine and feminine attributes of God.

Coming to the introduction of John's Gospel from such an approach road tunes us in to appreciate the mystery of the eternal Word. In one sense, it is so much an intrinsic part of the nature of God that it cannot be seen as separate from him, any more than his wisdom can. In another sense, Jesus the Christ is that Word separately enfleshed, visible to us when God remains hidden from our sight. There is clearly a link between personified Wisdom, of the

Hebrew tradition, and the personified eternal Word, which resonated with Greek thinking. The One who draws all this together is Christ, living out, in human person terms, the creative loving of God.

As Paul explains in his letter to the Christians at Colossae, God was dwelling in all his fullness in the person of Jesus, so that he alone was able to reconcile all to himself, healing the creative harmony which sin had ripped apart. The wisdom Christ displays, then, is of complete integrity and vulnerable love.

Sunday before Lent

Thought for the day
God's glory shows.

Reflection on the readings
2 Kings 2:1-12; Psalm 50:1-6
2 Corinthians 4:3-6; Mark 9:2-9

It is easy to understand why, since ancient times, people have worshipped the sun. Quite apart from its dazzling beauty, and its faithfulness in appearing each morning, all living things seem to sense that they depend on the sun for survival. Plants grow their first tentative shoots towards it, and adjust their flowering according to the length of day-light. Many flowers turn their heads to follow the sun's progress through the day, and all the complexities of animal and plant activity are locked into their relationship with our nearest star. Earth and the other planets in the solar system owe their very development to it.

So it is not surprising that sunlike images of fire and light are frequently used to describe the presence of the living God – images which speak of power, essence of life, sustaining support, faithfulness and beauty that hurts when we look at it directly. Or we can look at it from the other direction and see how God inevitably displays his nature in his creation, and it says a lot about him that the very first word of creation was 'Let there be light!' Creating the sunlight, and a teeming planet's life depending on it, was providing us with clues about the energising Creator, and our dependence on him.

It certainly feels entirely appropriate that God's glory, being seen in Jesus as he is transfigured, shows him being lit up, bright and seemingly pure. The people of Israel had in their communal history many stories of fiery encounters with God, such as Moses' burning bush, the pillar of fire guiding and protecting them on their escape from Egypt, the extra person seen in the burning fiery furnace, and the heavenly chariots of fire as Elijah is taken from Elisha's sight. Today's Psalm is one of many expressing God as a consuming fire.

Mark's account of the transfiguration comes immediately after Jesus has been telling his disciples about his necessary suffering and death before he comes into glory. To help them cope with what is ahead they are allowed a fleeting glimpse of the holistic truth, where the glory is evident, so that when it is hidden in the horror of the cross, they may begin to understand what real glory involves.

First Sunday of Lent

Thought for the day

After his Baptism Jesus is led by the Spirit into the wilderness before returning to proclaim God's kingdom.

Reflection on the readings

Genesis 9:8-17; Psalm 25:1-10
1 Peter 3:18-22; Mark 1:9-15

Today we begin the season of Lent, committing the next six weeks to preparing ourselves for the festival of Resurrection by looking seriously at the implications of turning to God at our baptism. So it is appropriate to start at the point of Jesus' baptism filling him with God's Spirit and promptly driving him into a six-week ordeal of vocational testing and spiritual battling.

Jesus' ministry did not begin with warm glowing feelings but rigorous self-discipline, painful soul-searching and cost-counting. When he later spoke about our need to count the cost of discipleship he was talking from personal experience. Committing ourselves wholeheartedly to God's service is indeed a costly business, and one it is quite natural to back away from as we start to realise the full implications. Are we really willing to say to God, 'Thy will be done; thy kingdom come'? Wouldn't we far prefer it to be our will and kingdom with God's blessing! Most of us feel fine about obedience until it differs from what we want in life; at which point we start jumping up and down complaining about the unfairness of it all.

One of the precious, valuable things we can learn from Jesus' example is to recognise the conflicts as a valid part of the process. Jesus knew he had some difficult things to face, and he knew he would not be ready for his ministry until he had taken time out to face them squarely, however unpleasant that might be. All too often our reaction is to deny our fears and questions, or edit them before approaching God with them, as we consider them inappropriate prayer material.

But the truth is that God wants our real, honest selves, and can't start working in earnest with us until we are willing to share with him everything – and that includes misgivings, things which embarrass us to mention to anyone, recognition of things we had hoped for and dreamed about and which we dislike the idea of giving up. If there is anything we feel ashamed to mention to God, then that's probably the most important thing he wants us to say.

Of course, we are not going to come to any of this lightly or easily. We are wonderfully inventive when it comes to rewriting agendas we find threatening to us or prefer to ignore. That is why we all need a wilderness, and time to be alone with God, without distraction. The wilderness is honesty, and we need to get used to its bare and uncompromising landscape, where conflicts are bound to confront us, but from which we will emerge stronger and more integrated as people, ready to go out in God's power.

Noah and his family are at that point as the rainbow of God's saving promise marks the end of storms and floods, and they can walk as new people into a new landscape.

Second Sunday of Lent

Thought for the day

A commitment of faith has far-reaching implications.

Reflection on the readings

Genesis 17:1-7, 15-16; Psalm 22:23-31
Romans 4:13-25; Mark 8:31-38

The desert experience of Lent continues today with Jesus determined that his disciples should be fully aware of the implications of his true identity. Mark tells us that, immediately following their recognition of him as God's Messiah, he starts spelling out to them what this means, and how it differs from their dreams.

The God of truth insists on our knowing the truth, even if it might turn us against him or temporarily hurt us or upset our plans; never will he pander to our misguided longings – he has too much respect for us. Gently, but firmly and openly, Jesus outlines the real Messiah's role – a role in which suffering, rejection and death are inevitable.

Such apparent failure, though clearly explored in the scriptures, had been conveniently overwritten by the popular dream of a resistance fighter who would lead the victorious struggle against Roman oppression and occupation.

From Jesus' response to Peter's protests, it is clear that the horror of such a future can still tempt him to side-step what he is called to go through. The temptations Jesus had been facing in the desert are here flaring up again through the misguided well-wishing of his friend. Impressed by personal experience of the power of such temptations, Jesus gathers not only his disciples but all his followers in the area together, to prepare them as thoroughly and honestly as he can for such temptations in their own lives to side-step the will of God.

It is quite true – we shall be tempted, time and again, to take the easier route and thus avoid the conflicts which are bound to accompany committed discipleship. But if we go along with such temptations, where do we end up? Without any 'life' (in the fullest sense of the word) left to live. And, as Jesus suggests, isn't it better to have the wicked ashamed of us, rather than Jesus and the holy angels of God?

But how on earth do we manage to be strong enough to resist the pull of the world of comfort, personal safety and self-gratification? We are given the example of Abraham, whose faith kept him walking and thinking God's way, even when it did not look exactly promising. He trusted God so firmly that he stuck with it through thick and thin, and that is what delighted God.

Anyone is a child of Abraham who is a child of faith; and in no circumstance whatsoever will God ever let them down.

Third Sunday of Lent

Thought for the day

God's wisdom may shock us. Jesus, obedient to God's Law and fulfilling it, dies a death which, according to the Law, makes him cursed.

Reflection on the readings

Exodus 20:1-17; Psalm 19
1 Corinthians 1:18-25; John 2:13-22

Probably no one was more surprised at Jesus' behaviour in the temple than those sitting buying and selling there. It had become normal practice – a tradition even – for the marketing side of worship to flourish, and the petty corruption involved was something everyone had come to expect and live with. We all get used to our own dirt and scruffiness and stop noticing it after a while. But Jesus finds it highly offensive. Why?

One of the hallmarks of Jesus' life is obedience, born of attentive listening to his heavenly Father. Understanding the Father's longing and will urges him to work for its accomplishment on earth. Lack of obedience, on the other hand, is closely linked with the desire to act independently of God. Throughout the desert time of testing, Jesus drew great strength for resistance from his mature obedience to the words of God in scripture. He found, like the writer of Psalm 19, that 'the Law of the Lord is perfect, reviving the soul'. Jesus knew that he had come to fulfil the scriptures, and that full obedience, even when severely challenging, was the only way for this to happen.

In our own society there is very little of an obedience ethic, and a rather distorted image of obedience as being something mature people can grow out of as they achieve rational independence. So we find the whole idea of commandments rather heavy, and might even feel that the rights of those temple sellers need to be upheld against Jesus' action.

Jesus knows that our holiness will only develop in line with our obedience to God, and, if we casually break God's Law as if it doesn't matter, we will find ourselves weak and unable to withstand temptations when they come. For our own survival spiritually we have to be rigorous with ourselves. One of the benefits of this desert time of discipline in Lent is that we are strengthened.

What Jesus finds offensive is that God's temple, set apart to be a place of holiness and prayer, is filled instead with buying and selling, profit-making and cheating. Our bodies are temples of the Holy Spirit. Are they also filled with buying and selling, profit-making and cheating? And, if so, do we care that we are therefore being disobedient to God's Law? Does it occur to us that we would be stronger and better enabled to resist temptation if we were rather 'houses of prayer'?

Fourth Sunday of Lent: Mothering Sunday

Thought for the day

God provides comfort in all our troubles
and sufferings.

Reflection on the readings

Exodus 2:1-10 or 1 Samuel 1:20-28
Psalm 34:11-20 or Psalm 127:1-4
2 Corinthians 1:3-7 or Colossians 3:12-17
Luke 2:33-35 or John 19:25-27

Television advertisements would have us believe in a normal family life of immaculate mums smiling as their families appear with their best clothes filthy; of inept dads being shown up by their perfect wife-and-mother partners, and hideous children who rule the whole family by their tyrannical demands. It is not many years since we were fed normal families of laughing togetherness, combined with perfect fashion sense and model good looks, where dad ruled and everyone was happy.

The styles may change but what stays the same is the pressure of image. All the media brandish the latest image instructions, and the pressure is on to conform, with the implied carrot that living the image will lead to success. Strewn along the wayside are all the casualties – those who have struggled to achieve the impossible in an illusory competition.

Refreshingly, our readings for Mothering Sunday place us fairly and squarely in the real world. Here family life is the wonderful patchwork of bright and dark colours, glowing sections and dull areas that we all recognise. It includes troubles and tragedies that hit us between the eyes and send us reeling, and also those moments of tender comforting which have such power to heal and enable us to carry on.

What we are being reminded of is God's parenting, which is no false, demanding image, but the real thing – the parenting we all need for our survival, and crave, sensing its importance. Not that we always remember to come to God for it; all too often we search for it instead among fallible humanity, and find ourselves let down and abandoned as a result. As humans we bear a resemblance to God's parenting, but we are bound to let one another down sometimes. God's arms are the ones that embrace all of us, holding us all in those loving arms, mopping all our tears and setting us on our feet again.

We hear of terrible, tragic situations of heartache in today's readings, which are redeemed by God's parenting love. As Paul says, God is the one who comforts us in all our troubles. We don't have to pretend with God that there aren't any troubles, or that we're managing very nicely, thank you. God knows what family life is about – and single life. He knows the heartaches and the conflicts. He knows that loving makes us vulnerable.

That's why God is so well able to comfort us within our real situations, and enable us to cope with the ordinary troubles of life without being overwhelmed by them; he has the resources we need available and his arms are outstretched in welcome.

Fifth Sunday of Lent

Thought for the day

Through Christ's death, full life would come to people of
all nations and generations.

Reflection on the readings

Jeremiah 31:31-34; Psalm 51:1-12 or Psalm 119:9-16
Hebrews 5:5-10; John 12:20-33

The people of Israel had been advised to strap the Law to
their foreheads and around their doorposts in order to try
and keep God's rules always in mind, but Jeremiah looks
forward to a time when people will have God's Law deep
within them in a new and dynamic way. And it is with the
coming of Jesus that the prophecy can be fulfilled. With
Jesus Christ there in person, people can see and understand what God is like, and with God's Spirit poured into
their hearts, after Jesus' Ascension, the new and intimate
relationship with God becomes a reality for those in every
age and place.

In today's Gospel we are told by John that some Gentile
Greeks are actually seeking Jesus out. He had just finished
cleansing the temple so that it could be restored as a house
of prayer for all nations, and now here are representatives
of those other nations asking for him. With their coming, it
is as if Jesus suddenly catches sight of that future, rolling
out into the distance of time and space, with people of all
nations giving God glory and worshipping him in Spirit
and in truth. At the same time he recognises that his own
finger is poised on the button that will make it possible.
He is acutely aware of the necessary agony he must suffer
for it to happen, and, in his humanness, shrinks from that.

He battles with what we all know so well – the powerful human instinct to preserve ourselves and avoid pain and conflict. Being the Son of God did not immunise Jesus against the struggle of sacrifice. Gloriously, love triumphs, and Jesus relinquishes everything to the will and glory of God; it must be done, and willingly done.

Immediately and powerfully the Father's love affirms what he has chosen, and all in the crowd who have ears to hear, whether Jew or Gentile, hear that unity of loving will for the good of the whole world.

Palm Sunday

Thought for the day

As the Messiah, Jesus enters Jerusalem,
knowing that he rides towards rejection and death
in order to save his people.

Reflection on the readings

Liturgy of the Palms:
Mark 11:1-11 or John 12:12-16; Psalm 118:1-2, 19-24

Liturgy of the Passion:
Isaiah 50:4-9a; Psalm 31:9-16
Philippians 2:5-11
Mark 14:1-15:47 or Mark 15:1-39 (40-47)

Palm Sunday takes us through the great drama of what it means for Jesus to be the Messiah. This week, often named 'Holy Week', is the culmination and accomplishment of all the Law, prophets and history of the Bible. It's here that the promises make good, that the secrets of the kingdom are displayed, and that the truth of God's saving love is acted out. Just as at moments of crisis our brains click into a kind of slow motion where the events are crowded in, so the Gospels report this last week of Jesus' earthly life with all the detail and heightened perception of people witnessing to the most significant and important week ever.

As he comes into Jerusalem riding on a donkey, Jesus is choosing to act out, three-dimensionally, what he is. He does what the prophecies had said the Messiah would do, spelling out to everyone both his authority and his style of leadership. Donkeys are humble beasts of burden, and Jesus, son of King David both as family and as the anointed

One, is proclaiming that God's Messiah comes to his people as a servant King.

The only way we have any hope of grasping what this means is by going on to hear, as fully as possible, the extent to which the humility and obedience of this servanthood is taken. This enables us to see the waving palms and shouts of victory through the racking torture of the cross; and the seeming cursed failure of the cross through the waving palms and shouts of victory. Both are victory and both are sacrifice.

Mark's account of the Passion shows us a poignantly human Jesus, fully integrated with the frailty of human nature we are so familiar with ourselves. How he longs for it to be possible to avoid what he dreads, and how he needs support from his heavy-eyed and terrified disciples, who abandon him. Perhaps the most terrible part of the whole ordeal of the arrest, trial, torture and crucifixion, is that acute sense of utter abandonment, blocking him off even from his heavenly Father.

The liturgy of today shakes us and prepares us to travel with Jesus through this week of most costly loving.

Easter Day

Thought for the day

Jesus is alive; Love has won the victory
over sin and death.

Reflection on the readings

Acts 10:34-43 or Isaiah 25:6-9; Psalm 118:1-2, 14-24
1 Corinthians 15:1-11 or Acts 10:34-43
John 20:1-18 or Mark 16:1-8

So the unavoidable, total sacrifice was given, along with all its pain and suffering which Jesus had dreaded. Through rejection, brutal torture and utter abandonment, Love held strong and refused to be conquered by the worst that evil and sin could throw at it. It took the Lord of life deep into the darkness of death, so that even that journey, which we must all make alone, is graced for ever with his presence. Left behind, stunned and shaken, the followers and friends of Jesus don't know what to think about anything any more.

And now, on the third day after his death, the impossible happens, and Jesus returns to life. It isn't the same kind of life, of course – how could it be with that journey behind him? Death has taken him beyond ordinary human life. God's loving power has drawn him out of death into the 'entirety life' which is completely full and has no limits either of time or space.

In the Gospel accounts of the Resurrection we are constantly aware of the struggle people had with accepting that Jesus was really with them again. Whenever we are faced with amazing good news, we find it almost 'too good to be true', and these first fragmentary meetings with the risen Jesus are often as much filled with terror and confusion as joy.

Jesus lets them take their time to grasp the reality of what has happened. Patiently he explains the scriptures, eats with them and loves them, until it dawns on them that, although it is so extraordinary and so wonderful, they can believe it – because it's true.

Second Sunday of Easter

Thought for the day

Our faith in the risen Christ
is bound to affect the way we live.

Reflection on the readings

Acts 4:32-35; Psalm 133
1 John 1:1-2:2; John 20:19-31

If we are travelling along dark roads at night and trust the road surface, we probably drive quite quickly and confidently, whereas driving along a road we know to be full of potholes is a matter of gingerly approaching and peering, so as to avoid damaging us or the car. What we believe affects the way we behave.

On this second Sunday of Easter the readings lead us to recognise that belief in a risen crucified Christ is bound to change things. With the Resurrection we know, more completely than ever before, that God is to be trusted, God is light without any darkness at all, and, what is more, we can share in that companionship of light and freedom with the living God.

In the reading from Acts we are shown a few snapshots of how this was worked out in practice for the early believers. We find them united in a common purpose, without in-house arguments, and free of possessiveness; individual belongings no longer seem important to them as their concern for one another's needs has taken over. Central to all this is the fact that they are still excited and amazed by the Resurrection; they are conscious of the risen Jesus living among them in person.

Do we, as a Christian community, live in that conviction, or has the Resurrection, over the years, turned into history for us? As we reflect on these Easter readings, they can light up our faith again; rather like turning up the thermostat on the heating, so that instead of just the quiet, steady pilot light burning away, the whole boiler flames into action. The risen Jesus walks into any gathering in any age, even those who have locked themselves in. And the meeting with Thomas, a week after the others have met with Jesus, shows us clearly that he is quite prepared to start with us where we are, addressing our particular fears, doubts and misgivings and leading us at a pace we can cope with, into the fullness of faith.

Third Sunday of Easter

Thought for the day

Having redeemed us by his death, Jesus can offer us the
forgiveness of our sin, which sets us free to live.

Reflection on the readings

Acts 3:12-19; Psalm 4
1 John 3:1-7; Luke 24:36b-48

The Gospel for today recounts the events of that first Sunday
evening after the crucifixion, when Jesus was suddenly there
in person among his terrified disciples, putting their fears to
rest, directing them to tell people they can be forgiven, and
forgiving them in the name of the risen Christ. Of all the
things Jesus might have said to his disciples on these brief
encounters from life beyond death, why does he focus on
repentance and forgiveness?

Surely because something had happened during those
hours of agony on the cross, and at the moment of dying,
which changed things for ever. We are told that the curtain
of the temple ripped from top to bottom, a symbolic tearing
down of the barrier of sin between God and his people; and
now, from the perspective of the Resurrection, Jesus passes
on to his disciples the urgent work of tearing down that
barrier wherever it exists, in every person of all time.

In the reading from Acts we see Peter doing exactly what
Jesus had said. Using every opportunity – in this case the
people's amazement at the healing of the man unable to
walk – he directs their attention to the real power and the
powerful reality. It is through Jesus that the man is healed.
This leads them straight on to the spiritual 'setting free' of
repentance and forgiveness which is now available.

John, too, speaks from the viewpoint of one who knows what a difference it makes to be set free like this; the extent of God's love which makes such an enriched life possible still amazes him. It isn't a one-off operation, this forgiveness, though it often starts with a dramatic change of life direction. But we need to come regularly before the throne of God with humility to voice our sin, and our longing to be forgiven, and to experience that cleansing and refreshing which comes from God's acceptance and forgiveness.

In fact, as our relationship with the living Jesus deepens, we shall find it increasingly uncomfortable to carry on in a state of sin without going to God to have it lifted from us, so as to restore us once again to that marvellous freedom we have experienced before. It is God's longing that all his humanity should be able to share the liberating joy of repenting and being forgiven. Knowing what we are all missing out on by lugging our sin around, and living only the 'till death' kind of life, Jesus sees repentance and forgiveness as urgent priorities for us – the stuff of a new order; the stuff of God's kingdom.

Fourth Sunday of Easter

Thought for the day

'I am the Good Shepherd
and I lay down my life for the sheep.'

Reflection on the readings

Acts 4:5-12; Psalm 23
1 John 3:16-24; John 10:11-18

Being imprisoned for the night may not look much like an opportunity, but in fact it provides the perfect opening for Peter and John to speak out about the power of Jesus who, though crucified, is now alive for ever. We heard last week how they had already been able to use healing to preach the good news to the crowds, bringing the number of believers to about five thousand. Just as Jesus had said would happen, they are given the words to say when asked to bear witness to the truth.

It is quite easy, of course, to make a point of not talking much to God about being given opportunities (in case he takes us up on it!) and to ignore or side-step such opportunities when they do happen. All too glibly do we persuade ourselves that we are not meant to force-feed people, or put them off by actually talking about God's involvement with lives and events. Certainly ramming God down people's throats is both unloving and counter-productive. But there is a great danger of using this as an excuse for avoiding the work we are commissioned to do, in many situations where people lose out on the blessings of forgiveness God longs for them to enjoy, simply because we chicken out of passing on the good news.

In today's Gospel, we hear the well-loved and treasured words of Jesus, describing himself as the Good Shepherd, the one who gathers the flock and tends the sheep, looking after their needs and leading them safely. In contrast to the hired worker, the authentic shepherd is even prepared to lay down his own life for the protection of the sheep. And that is good news worth passing on, at whatever cost to us. John reflects on what it means, and how it expresses incredible love – the willingness to lay down one's life for one's friends.

Quite importantly, it makes clear that Jesus was not forced into dying; it would have been possible to avoid it, right up to the very last breath. There had been the temptation to do so at intervals throughout his ministry, and even as he hung dying he was goaded to 'show his power' by coming down from the cross. It was, then, at the moments of greatest weakness that Jesus actually showed his greatest strength of love.

And that is often true for us as well. Weakness feels just that; without glamour or nobility or anything other than the recognition that we have no strength of ourselves to do any more; yet it is in living through such times in God's strength that others turn out to be blessed and God's name to be glorified. If only we will trust God at such times, who knows what sheep will be rescued?

Fifth Sunday of Easter

Thought for the day

To produce fruit we need to be joined on to the true vine.

Reflection on the readings

Acts 8:26-40; Psalm 22:25-31
1 John 4:7-21; John 15:1-8

This week the reading from Acts continues the Spirit-led proclaiming of the good news, once again following the same pattern given by the risen Jesus during his encounters with the disciples. Philip arrives at the right place at the right time, because he has been closely in touch with God's leading. He tunes into the Ethiopian official's questions and seeking after truth, and explains who Jesus is and why he died, using the scriptures and interpreting them in the light of the Resurrection. It is all to do with working co-operatively with God, and allowing respect and love for one another to sensitise us to people's real needs, even if these are confused and unvoiced.

What happened to the Ethiopian as a result of this encounter? We only know that he went on his way rejoicing; probably he carried on the broadcasting of the good news, so that many others were also set free to live rejoicing lives.

The elderly John is still marvelling at the way God loves us, and is anxious to make it quite clear that double standards on our part will not do. Faced with the beauty of God's perfect love, it is no good claiming to love him if we are full of hate for another human being. Real love of God is bound to lead us on to love one another in the same tender, unselfish way that he loves us.

This is why the image of the vine and branches is such a vivid and useful one; being joined on to the vine makes all the difference, and we cannot expect to produce spiritual fruit unless we are well attached, with the life sap flowing through us. Jesus places himself in the role of vine and his Father as the gardener. Why does a gardener plant a vine and tend it? For the fruit! What a thought it is to imagine wine made from the fruit of our love, joy, peace, patience, kindness, goodness, faithfulness, gentleness and self-control, all possible because of the life of Jesus flowing through our living and growing. Wine of the kingdom of God.

Sixth Sunday of Easter

Thought for the day

We are to love one another as Jesus loves us.

Reflection on the readings

Acts 10:44-48; Psalm 98
1 John 5:1-6; John 15:9-17

In the reading from Acts we witness an extraordinary out-pouring of the Holy Spirit, which doesn't even wait for Peter to finish speaking. Not surprisingly, when you look back to what he had just been saying, you find once again that powerful truth about forgiveness, which Jesus had commissioned his disciples to tell everyone about. 'Tell them they can be forgiven,' he had said straight after the Resurrection. As Peter proclaims this, the little crowd of people in Cornelius' house, who are searching single-mindedly for God's truth, suddenly experience the rush of God's forgiving love, and the freedom it brings.

And this is the kind of love we are given as an example to follow – the kind of forgiving, accepting love that wants people to be free. So much of what we name as love is actually to do with self-gratification and possession. It is tied up with our own need for fulfilment. But the love that Jesus talks of in today's Gospel is about obedience, willing co-operation, and sacrifice which produces joy.

There is a danger of mishearing what Jesus means here. He is not saying that in order to be his beloved friends we have to obey his commands. That would be fine if we could earn God's love by clocking up the points, and many people conscientiously live like this. But it does not set them free. It was because we can't earn God's blessing that we needed a

Saviour to give us freely the forgiveness which liberates us to live; and it is because God has treated us with such love and respect and generosity that, as his friends, we take delight in obeying his commands and living the loving way.

Jesus doesn't want to have us as servants, who obey because it's their job but know nothing of their employer's business. He has gone out of his way to involve us at every stage, pointing out the policies and plans, and the 'mission statement'. That makes us more like friends and colleagues with the God of creation, which is a heady prospect and also quite a responsibility.

Ascension Day

Thought for the day

Having bought back our freedom with the giving of his life, Jesus enters into the full glory to which he is entitled.

Reflection on the readings

Acts 1:1-11 or Daniel 7:9-14; Psalm 47 or Psalm 93
Ephesians 1:15-23 or Acts 1:1-11; Luke 24:44-53

The disciples have walked with Jesus on his journey to the cross, watched his suffering there and known the darkness of that time, then met him full of Resurrection life on various recorded occasions since Easter. During these encounters they have gradually begun to understand God's purposes and are getting used to knowing Jesus' constant presence, whether they can actually see him with them or not. And Jesus has accomplished all that he set out from heaven to do.

So the time has come for Jesus to move into the full glory of heaven, united with his Father and given his rightful place. In a sense the Ascension is like the completion of the Resurrection. Those post-Resurrection meetings were an essential part of the mission, preparation for the spread of the good news which could only be done after the victory over death.

When Jesus had met Mary of Magdala in the garden on that Sunday morning, he had told her not to hold him as he was not yet ascended to his Father. After his death, Jesus had preached to the dead, and now he was walking about among the living on earth. But this was not to be his permanent home. With the Ascension, Jesus is finally 'resurrected' into the glory of heaven for ever. He is also fully available to touch every life in a way never possible before.

No one witnessed the Resurrection, but now, with the promise of power to be sent on the disciples, they see Jesus taken up into heaven. We are reminded of Elisha, promised Elijah's power only if he was allowed to witness his master's parting from earth. And from now on until the Day of Pentecost, they wait in expectant obedience for the empowering of the Holy Spirit.

Today is one of those festivals which look in both directions at once. We look back over all that led up to Christ's coming, and over that earthly human sharing from the manger to the empty tomb; and we look forward to the spreading of the kingdom far and wide through space and time, empowered by the Spirit. As Emmanuel, 'God-with-us', bridges earth and heaven at the Ascension, the human is caught up in the divine for ever.

Seventh Sunday of Easter

Thought for the day

Although now hidden from our sight, Jesus lives for ever, and in him we can live the Resurrection life even while we are on earth.

Reflection on the readings

Acts 1:15-17, 21-26; Psalm 1
1 John 5:9-13; John 17:6-19

With the Ascension, the earthly ministry of Jesus drew to a close, with the prospect of God's Spirit flooding into the believers, so that in that power they would be enabled to spread the good news down the generations and out to every far-flung community on earth. In our reading from Acts we see the disciples growing up and taking their responsibility seriously, even before the empowering has taken place.

Already, we are told, there are about a hundred and fifty of them, and Peter is the leader. Their first job they see as choosing a Judas replacement, the main criterion being that the candidate should have been an eye-witness to the entire ministry of Jesus. Sensibly they pray for it to be God's choice – not 'help us to choose wisely' but 'show us who you have chosen'. That is an example well worth following.

The elderly John writes in his letter to remind his readers that the eternal life God gives us is invested in his Son, so it follows that those who accept Jesus as Lord will have that life, and those who reject him will not. We are into personal choices again.

Jesus, being human, well understands the kind of world we live in and the minefield of temptations we walk through.

As he prayed for his disciples, knowing that he would soon be physically parted from them, Jesus prayed for our protection from evil, and for a realistic harmony and unity. Looking around at our sects and splits, it is easy to see why Jesus was so concerned. Our witness to the glorious, liberating truth is so weakened by our disunity.

Thankfully, we live in an age which is doing its best to refocus on Jesus, so that the great barriers erected through the centuries between Christians may in time crumble to rubble. All this is the work of God's Spirit; the more God's people open themselves to receive that empowering love, the more able we will be to love one another, respecting one another's differences but recognising that we are fellow workers, indwelt by the same Spirit.

Pentecost

Thought for the day

The Holy Spirit of God is poured out in power on the
expectant disciples, just as Jesus promised.

Reflection on the readings

Acts 2:1-21 or Ezekiel 37:1-14; Psalm 104:24-34, 35b
Romans 8:22-27 or Acts 2:1-21; John 15:26-27; 16:4b-15

As humans we are quite a conservative bunch. Most of us
like to hold on to what we are familiar with; to 'our' way
of doing things. Since Easter, Jesus' disciples had been
learning to let go of the familiar presence of their teacher
and friend. He had assured them that he needed to leave
them for a while, so that he would be able to send them
the Spirit, but before the crucifixion this news had simply
made them miserable and threatened, filled with grief. All
they could see was a future without Jesus, a prospect that
knocked the bottom out of their world.

Now, today, we are celebrating, because we join with
the disciples as they are overwhelmed with joy. Whatever
they had imagined it would be like to receive God's Holy
Spirit, the actual experience hugely surpasses. Far from
feeling destitute without Jesus' presence, they now sense
him with them more deeply and closer than ever before.

All the things Jesus had patiently tried to explain to
them they can understand with a new clarity, as if the light
of God has suddenly been switched on in their thinking.
All Jesus' urgency for telling people the good news now
fills them with zeal they have never known before.

Suddenly the most important thing to do is communicate
God's love to those who don't know it. The ability to speak

in the different languages of the visitors to Jerusalem is all part of this newly given love for people which cannot wait to let them in on the secret of real freedom. The Holy Spirit, coming like flame, sets the disciples' hearts on fire with love for God and for other people.

No wonder Peter sees in all this the fulfilling of Joel's prophecy; suddenly it all falls logically into place. He realises that they are experiencing the first wave of a new age, with God's Spirit flooding out into those of all nations; God living in his people in a dynamic, revolutionary way. The offer is available to anyone genuinely desiring more of the living God in their lives.

Trinity Sunday

Thought for the day

The mysterious and holy nature of the one true God
is beyond our understanding, but it is both communal
harmony and individual personality,
Father, Son and Holy Spirit.

Reflection on the readings

Isaiah 6:1-8; Psalm 29
Romans 8:12-17; John 3:1-17

The festival of Trinity allows us time in the Church year to contemplate the nature of God, and marvel at it. One thing we shall never be able to do, as humans, is to grasp it with full understanding, simply because God is not made in our likeness, but we in his. Often people shrug off the possibility of God because he does not behave according to the limitations of humankind, and they feel he ought to if he is real.

God's reality is of a nature we cannot quantify and contain, rather as our eyes can only perceive certain colours in the rainbow while others are beyond our powers of vision. Isaiah's glimpse of God's holiness and glory is more in the realm of sensing than understanding, and with us, too, the moments when we become fleetingly aware of the depths of God's nature are probably moments of sense and inner assurance, rather than quantifiable knowledge. This is not something to worry about but rejoice in; no matter how much we discover to love and worship in the living God, there will always be the joy of more to explore and other treasure to find, and we can delight in the discovering.

As soon as we try to nail God down mathematically, we are bound to run into trouble, and the concept of the Trinity reminds us that all our models and shapes are only rough guides to help us; the reality is always more and different.

What we do know is that there is more to this life than the seen. As Jesus was helping Nicodemus to understand, even in the seen world there are invisible things like wind. How much more when we are in the realm of the Spirit. If we are open to the possibility of it being so, we shall start to notice it. It's actually the Spirit 'in line' with our spirit which makes the necessary connections.

One of the glorious things about people is their wholesome loathing of being fobbed off with lies as the truth. The Spirit leads us into truth, and God is Truth, so we cannot seek Reality and Ultimate Truth without travelling deeper into the nature of the one true living God. The Son leads us to the Father and the Spirit; the Father leads us to listen to the Son and the Spirit; and the Spirit leads us to the Son and the Father.

Proper 4

Sunday between 29 May and 4 June inclusive
(if after Trinity Sunday)

Thought for the day

Jesus has the words of eternal life –
he sheds light on a right attitude to the Law.

Reflection on the readings

1 Samuel 3:1-10 (11-20) or Deuteronomy 5:12-15
Psalm 139:1-6, 13-18 or Psalm 81:1-10
2 Corinthians 4:5-12; Mark 2:23-3:6

The satisfying thing about rules is that we can achieve a
great sense of accomplishment when we have ticked them
all off. The accompanying danger is that they can lull us
into thinking we have done all that is necessary, simply
because we have kept the letter of the law. The spirit of the
law is far more open-ended, and cannot 'button up' our
ethics in the same way at all.

Today's readings blow fresh air into the stale and hollow
rule system which the sacred Law had become. In the
reading from Samuel we find God choosing to call to a
responsive child in a corrupt religious atmosphere in
order to shake things to life again, and in today's Gospel
we have instances of Jesus showing by example the Law
lit from God's perspective.

The keeping of the Sabbath was considered so important
that intricate, detailed rules had been built up around it, till
the sense of spending the day celebrating the good creation
and joyfully worshipping the Creator was choked in small-
print regulations. Jesus directs them to see it again as it
really is. He asks them whether it is lawful to do good or

evil on the Sabbath, which only allows the positive reply of actively doing good. To be tied down so tightly to the rules that your compassion has to be stamped on, can hardly be in keeping with the generous, caring Lord of Love.

This contrasted with the current thinking, which would probably have let the man's hand stay withered till the Sabbath rest was over. Jesus was not cancelling out the Law, or changing it; he was guiding his listeners back to its original freshness, and recognising that the whole Law is really about building a right and living relationship with God – loving God and loving one another.

In the reading from 2 Corinthians we are given a worked-out example of living by the Law lit up Jesus' way, with the full glory of God. What does such a life look like? We are shown a picture of extraordinary inner joy and vigour in spite of all the hardships and conflicts, dangers and threats. What is obvious is that these lives, rooted in God's grace, are not hemmed in but set free. Jesus has the words of eternal life, valid while we are still living here.

Proper 5

Sunday between 5 and 11 June inclusive
(if after Trinity Sunday)

Thought for the day

Anyone who does God's will
is considered a close family member of Jesus.

Reflection on the readings

1 Samuel 8:4-11 (12-15) 16-20 (11:14-15) or Genesis 3:8-15
Psalm 138 or Psalm 130
2 Corinthians 4:13-5:1; Mark 3:20-35

The terrible thing about sin is the rift and separation it causes between people, and between God and his people. As a result of Adam and Eve's wilful disobedience, the natural relationship between the Creator and his beloved creation goes horribly wrong, and they are no longer comfortable in God's presence, but hiding from him. So much self-deceit, hidden agendas and complicated destructive living is really to do with this hiding of ourselves from God. So much of Jesus' teaching was showing people how to feel comfortable in God's presence once again.

We see the same, typical human wilfulness in the reading from 1 Samuel, where the people's desire to be like all the other nations and have a king drives them to go against God's will in the matter. And we can all think of wilfulness in our own lives which has resulted in trouble for us and others.

Jesus is the great rift-healer. As Paul writes in 2 Corinthians, there is an ongoing healing for those who live in Christ, which renews us spiritually even as our physical bodies are wearing out. With the eyes of a professional tentmaker he sees physical death as merely a folding-up of one's tent, which has provided temporary accommodation during our journey through earthly life. The permanent house is a spiritual one, prepared for us in God's heaven. Paul adjusts our view to revel in the marvellous reality of what is unseen, rather than wasting time concentrating our attention only on the seen, temporary world.

At first sight today's Gospel does not look like Jesus in healing mode at all. He is being spoken of as using demonic powers to set people free from demons, and his family is concerned for his sanity, hearing the reports about him. These are very serious accusations and Jesus treats them seriously. To be God's chosen One, living out God's love, yet accused of being Love's destroyer, must have given Jesus intense, sharp pain. Surely this was all part of the sword Simeon had predicted, and here is Mary sharing it, just as he said she would.

As Jesus looks into the eyes of those around him, in that typical, straight encounter with people and affection for them, he is cherishing the wideness of close family. In God's love, our family extends and is no longer tied simply to blood and genes. Spiritually we are bound together in God's great family, as close to Jesus as his own flesh and blood.

Proper 6

Sunday between 12 and 18 June inclusive
(if after Trinity Sunday)

Thought for the day
From small beginnings, and by God's power,
the kingdom of heaven grows.

Reflection on the readings
1 Samuel 15:34-16:13 or Ezekiel 17:22-24
Psalm 20 or Psalm 92:1-4, 12-15
2 Corinthians 5:6-10 (11-13) 14-17; Mark 4:26-34

One of the things we all find difficult to do is relinquish power. We may consider that we don't possess much of that commodity, but just listen to yourself and others protesting as soon as our own way of doing something is challenged, or things are suddenly changed without us being told or even our opinion being asked. We bridle! Today's readings remind us that God is in charge, and can work in all kinds of ways and through all kinds of people whom we may not choose. He goes on working even when we are on holiday, ill, or asleep; though we are important in the growth of the kingdom, the whole thing will not fall apart whenever we are not personally involved. Today we are challenged to recognise that the growth of the kingdom of heaven is not entirely down to our conscientious activity, and we can and should let go and let God.

Samuel was wanting to hang on to Plan A for all kinds of good reasons, but God rouses him to move on in a fresh direction and anoint a new king of Israel. The nudge is sufficient, since Samuel is attentive, but sometimes we seem to need something far more explosive than a nudge before we'll give up on dead issues and agree instead to go God's way forward.

The reading from Ezekiel shows us God acting with typical care and forward planning in a dynamic new way. In contrast to Nebuchadnezzar's worldly empire building, God acts with deep wisdom, startling diversity and breadth of vision, and the power rather like that of a superb orchestra playing softly. God has his power under control and uses it with perfect love and integrity.

Extraordinary as it may seem, we can share in that. As Paul points out in 2 Corinthians, everyone was included in Christ's death so that everyone can also be included in his resurrection life, where our whole focus and aim runs in line with what God wants and longs for.

The seed in today's parable does not rely on the farmer's constant attention – it is quite capable of growing wonderfully on its own, simply because it is living seed. Whenever we sow the seed of God's love or his Word in someone's heart, God will continue his work of growth there, using all the circumstances of that person's experience to develop the growing. And what begins so small can grow beyond our imagining. We must never forget that all growth is God's doing. As Christians we are not in the business of empire-building for Christ, but praying for God's kingdom to come.

Proper 7

Thought for the day

What kind of person is this?
Even the wind and waves obey him.

Reflection on the readings

1 Samuel 17:(1a, 4-11, 19-23) 32-49 or
1 Samuel 17:57-18:5, 10-16 or Job 38:1-11
Psalm 9:9-20 or Psalm 133 or Psalm 107:1-3, 23-32
2 Corinthians 6:1-13; Mark 4:35-41

Although we perhaps know that God is all-mighty, the way we live often shows that we don't take this terribly seriously. Many claiming belief in God speak of him as a slightly ridiculous, inept but well-meaning gentleman, part security blanket and part Father Christmas. Any God with real power, many believe, would act to prevent pain and suffering, and design creation differently so that things didn't go wrong. For the most part God is ignored, much of the time even by his supposed friends and worshippers, and we live our daily lives with an occasional glance in God's direction. Praying is generally the last resort – 'All we can do now is pray'.

Today's readings bring us the shock of ordinary people brought suddenly into close contact with God's power in their ordinary lives. In the Gospel the disciples are floating in their solid, wooden-hulled fishing boat, with its smell of salt, damp and stale fish. The stained and wet sails are straining under the increasing wind, and the ropes creaking. All so normal and familiar.

But as the power of wind and waves increases out of control, and Jesus is woken up in their anxious panic, they suddenly witness a much greater power and authority than anything in the created world. The dramatically hushed and tamed sailing conditions shock the disciples into new questions about Jesus' full identity; they have just witnessed God's power in action, and it shakes them.

Other examples have been shown to us today in the Old Testament reading, of God demonstrating his power and authority. Whenever people glimpse it, they are brought to a new reverence and respect for God, as they suddenly see him in all his awesome greatness, and our condescending, human-sized impressions of him are shown up to be shamefully inappropriate.

The continued readings from 2 Corinthians show us Paul, still dazed from his encounter with the living Jesus, recognising the miracle of God's vitality and power working in the ordinariness of human beings, and the extraordinary effect of this in people's lives. It is, after all, a universe-builder we're talking about, an all-knowing, all-seeing God, whose reality should bring us frequently to our knees in utter wonder and adoration.

Proper 8

Thought for the day

God's power can reach even into death
and draw out life.

Reflection on the readings

2 Samuel 1:1, 17-27 or
Wisdom of Solomon 1:13-15; 2:23-24
Psalm 130 or Psalm 30 or Lamentations 3:23-33
2 Corinthians 8:7-15; Mark 5:21-43

(Lamentations 3:23-33 may be read as the first reading
in place of the Wisdom passage.)

Everything about death looks final. The body we knew
laughing, anxious, angry or intrigued is stilled; all the mem-
ories and stories locked inside and out of our reach. It seems
to be the end of responding, thinking, feeling and moving.
Clustered around it are other endings – the cupboards to be
cleared, possessions and clothing now redundant; terrible
gaps in family, friendships, committees and rotas, the particular pew. The tragedy of death is its terrible finality – it is
like a violent rejection of what was previously so very much
alive; a slap in the face to life itself. With King David, our
gut reaction to death is the grieving of endings – 'Look how
the mighty are fallen'.

Yet with God walking this planet in person as Jesus, we
discover in his ministry several cases of death's finality
being challenged and reversed. Jairus' twelve-year-old
daughter had left the living world and yet Jesus speaks into
death and calls her out of it, back into the world of life
again. She hears his call to her ('Talitha, koum!') and follows

it through a journey we can only imagine, emerging to stand up in the world she had left, no longer full of fever as before, but in full health and very hungry.

As with last week's miracle, we might ask why, if Jesus' compassion drove him to do such acts contrary to nature then, does he not continue to reverse natural laws daily and universally on grounds of compassion today? In fact, of course, there must have been many hundreds of other people dying during Jesus' ministry on earth, none of whom were raised from the dead. There are other reasons for Jesus acting like this in these particular situations; reasons to do with signs and pointers to Jesus' true identity.

But we are also challenged by the great faith shown in today's Gospel. In Jesus' encounter with the woman in the crowd, finally healed after twelve years of miserable ill health and uncleanness, according to the law, she is told that it is her faith which has healed her, even though Jesus knows that power has gone out of him. Did her faith draw that healing power out?

Certainly we do need to be expectant, considering God-incidences perfectly possible, allowing God permission for his kingdom to be unleashed in each situation. We choose whether or not to unbolt the door from the inside.

Proper 9

Thought for the day

If we are not ready to listen to the truth
we will not hear it.

Reflection on the readings

2 Samuel 5:1-5, 9-10 or Ezekiel 2:1-5
Psalm 48 or Psalm 123
2 Corinthians 12:2-10; Mark 6:1-13

Discreet rebellion does not go unnoticed by God. Whatever we proclaim with our lips, whatever we claim to believe, and however cleverly we disguise our rebellion from others, God sees and knows where our hearts really are, and which way we are really facing. This isn't something to make us scared of approaching God. It's actually quite a relief to find there's no point in pretending or trying to impress him. Those who, like me, tend to live in a certain amount of clutter, know there are some people whose visits spur us to a spate of frantic tidying, and others who know us so well that this isn't really necessary – they know and love us well exactly as we are!

When God has something to say to us which may involve opening us up more to his grace, challenging a fixed or self-centred attitude or behaviour, or a little spiritual growing-up, then he will tell us. But if we aren't ready or prepared to hear what he has to say, then there's no way we'll hear it. Later we might look back and wonder why we couldn't see the obvious! But at the time we're far more likely to react with hostility and defensiveness, rather like those in Jesus' home town. We can hear their indignant, self-righteous wounded egos as they mutter their complaints about Jesus. When they look at the facts, he's not even on a level with them for background; so what right has he to be displaying more wisdom and miracle-working than any of them? It is quite usual to resent holiness, or any other gift, in those close to us – holiness in strangers is far easier to cope with as we don't take that as personal criticism.

When Jesus sends out his disciples it is in the support of pairs, and, like Ezekiel, they are to preach repentance, whether the people are ready to listen or not. God had prepared Ezekiel for the likelihood of stubborn rebellious natures not taking kindly to the challenge, and now Jesus prepares his disciples in a similar way.

Brushing the dust from their feet is not a vindictive move, but a visual sign – a testimony – that the Gospel of repentance has been offered and refused. It is also important from the disciples' point of view, and ours. There are times when it is right to move on and leave the Holy Spirit to continue working in people's hearts through the subsequent events and conversations, without feeling weighed down by the rejection.

Proper 10

Thought for the day

Those who speak out God's will
are bound to be vulnerable to rejection and abuse.

Reflection on the readings

2 Samuel 6:1-5, 12b-19 or Amos 7:7-15
Psalm 24 or Psalm 85:8-13
Ephesians 1:3-14; Mark 6:14-29

Today's readings pulverise any suspicions we might have had that walking God's way is the comfortable option for wimps. We hear story after story of the reality – that those who speak out God's will are quite likely to find themselves rejected and abused, insulted and scorned. Perhaps Bibles should have a safety warning pasted on the front cover: 'Following the God you meet through these pages is usually dangerous.'

We hear of King David dancing with all his might before the Lord in an uninhibited outpouring of love and worship to God as the holy ark is brought into Jerusalem. The glamorous Michal's scorn as she watches him will sound familiar to many of our young Christians at school and university, who often have to suffer the pitying scorn of the glamorous because of their faith. They badly need our constant prayer support and encouragement.

We hear of Amos, told to push off and go back to his farming because he spoke out a message from God which his listeners did not want to hear. Never mind how right and wise God's advice is, those brave enough to speak it, when a community or a relationship needs changing, are bound to be treated as attackers, and are frequently fended off aggressively, at least initially. As a species we do not take criticism positively, but beat it off at all costs, even though it can help us grow. It is a mark of great maturity to be able to welcome criticism in order to learn from it.

In today's Gospel we find John the Baptist has been speaking out that dangerous truth to Herod, pointing out what God's will is and is not. Herod is pulled in two directions – both towards a liberating eternal relationship with the living God, and towards the personal power, wealth, gratification and popularity which spell short-term satisfaction and death. It is the latter he chooses, urged on by Herodias' aggressive resentment at John's meddling in their lives. Yet although John has been beheaded as a true prophet for faithfully speaking out God's word, the disciples are scattered over the countryside in pairs, preaching repentance and the kingdom for all they are worth!

We need to pray for the courage to speak out as God's people, and get on with the work we have been chosen to do, however we are received. All too often the first hint of opposition or waning popularity shuts us up, and we persuade ourselves that we shouldn't mention such things again. But if the early Church had followed a similar line, how many of us would ever have heard the good news of God's love?

Proper 11

Thought for the day

Like a good shepherd, Jesus sees the needs of his people
and always responds with love.

Reflection on the readings

2 Samuel 7:1-14a or Jeremiah 23:1-6
Psalm 89:20-37 or Psalm 23
Ephesians 2:11-22; Mark 6:30-34, 53-56

In the reading from 1 Samuel we find the shepherd King of Israel wanting to establish a permanent resting-place for the ark of the Covenant. In a gentle and gracious 'no', God affirms his love and protection of David and of his people during their nomadic history, and his promise of continued leadership and guidance right through into the future. The reading from Jeremiah, in contrast, shows God lamenting the destructive effect of bad leadership of his chosen people. As he sees them scattering in all directions, confused and undisciplined, the promise is made of the plan to draw them back under wholesome leadership, into the peace and settled spirit of God's charge.

In today's section of the letter to the Christians in Ephesus, Paul sets out the important aspect of Jesus' leadership: the breaking down of barriers between people, and the drawing together of those from different traditions and backgrounds into unity through the Christ.

Then in the Gospel we find Jesus doing just that, his heart of God aching to see the vulnerability of the crowds. In Jesus the image of the good shepherd king becomes a practical reality, and the people sense it, watching his every move, racing ahead of the boat to be at the other side of the lake when he arrives, ceaselessly demanding as they recognise their need of healing at all levels. They gravitate to the one whose words and works make contact with their deep, unconscious drive to be at one with the living God.

How does the humanness of Jesus cope with such over-whelming demands? Loving with God's love makes him responsive without reserve, and he is never recorded in the Gospels as turning anyone away. However, he is obviously aware of his human need for rest and refreshment, and we do pick up on the weariness and exhaustion of ministry on such a scale. His early morning walks into the hills for solitary prayer are vital to him, and there is evidence that part of his leadership responsibility was aiming to provide periods of rest and retreat for his close disciples and him-self. Presumably there were at least some occasions when they managed these oases of quiet, without the crowds catching up with them!

All this enables us to look at the question of demands in ministry, and the provision we make for our own leaders' spiritual refreshment and quiet reflection. We need to look both at the extent of our willingness to put ourselves out for others, and also at the dangers of overworking with insufficient support or rest. We are challenged to see the way crowds naturally flock to where they sense God being proclaimed in the person of Jesus, and check that visitors to our churches are enabled to meet with the living Christ there.

Proper 12

Thought for the day

Out of God's riches, a great crowd is fed and satisfied
from a small offering of food.

Reflection on the readings

2 Samuel 11:1-15 or 2 Kings 4:42-44
Psalm 14 or Psalm 145:10-18
Ephesians 3:14-21; John 6:1-21

Great evil and great good do not simply happen out of the
blue; both begin in small, barely noticed incidents, whose
significance only becomes apparent once the evil or goodness has snowballed. King David had for some reason
stayed at home instead of leading his army, when he saw
Bathsheba bathing, and from these seemingly little events
the sin accumulated. Huge international conflicts can be
traced back to a number of small-scale wrongs or misguided
attitudes, or an early absence of real communication.

Thankfully the same is true of goodness, and today we
are celebrating the way that small acts of generosity and
love can be blessed and transformed for great, widespread
good. It is like watching a parable of the growth of the
kingdom of heaven in action.

First we read about the distribution of twenty barley
loaves among a hundred people – a combination of one
man's generosity and Elisha's close and faithful relationship with God – so close that he can discern God's will and
acts obediently. As a result, many more people are blessed
by the original gift than could have been imagined.

The reading from Ephesians reinforces this lavish
nature of God's provision. Paul knows from experience

that with his power working in us God can do so much more than anything we can ask or imagine, and Paul longs for his readers to take this on board so that they too can live in the fulfilment of God's faithful promises.

In today's Gospel one boy's offer of lunch is accepted with thanks, blessed and used so that thousands are fed. It is always a temptation to look at huge needs and dismiss what we are able to do as being pathetically inadequate so that we end up being too discouraged even to use what we do have. The work of Mother Theresa was sometimes dismissed as being too little to make any difference, but, as far as she was concerned, every little act of loving kindness was something beautiful for God, and infinitely worth doing. That 'little' has been so greatly blessed and brought hope and joy to so many all over the world.

Each of us has a lifetime's worth of moments to offer, each very small but each there to give. Anything that we offer for God to use, however small or insignificant it may seem to be, is gathered up, blessed and redistributed for blessing beyond our imagining.

Proper 13

Thought for the day

Jesus is the Bread of Life who satisfies our hunger and
sustains us on our journey to heaven.

Reflection on the readings

2 Samuel 11:26-12:13a or Exodus 16:2-4, 9-15
Psalm 51:1-12 or Psalm 78:23-29
Ephesians 4:1-16; John 6:24-35

In our Exodus reading the people were finding their
hunger dampening their pioneering spirit considerably,
and the provision of quails and manna saved the day, as
well as proclaiming God's care for his people.

Most of us start getting irritable and short-tempered
when our bodies need food. Complicated or demanding
decisions are always best left till after a meal, rather than
trying to rush into them when we return home weary and
hungry, and in mountain-climbing the hot drinks and food
are first on the agenda when setting up camp at the end of
the day. We are all deeply affected by the appalling sight of
real hunger and starvation. Since we all have bodies which
run on the fuel of food, we all instinctively know the
importance of feeding, right from screaming our hunger at
birth. Food is simply a matter of life and death.

This makes it an ideal image for describing how important Jesus is to us. When he says, 'I am the Bread of Life', we
understand the life and death nature of the relationship; it
implies that Jesus brings us life, and without him we die.
That is why it is linked with the Resurrection – the risen
nature of Christ. All we are to do is believe in Jesus and we

will be taken with him through death into the fullness of life with God for ever. Believing is attaching ourselves to him so that wherever Jesus goes we end up being taken as well.

What saddened Jesus in today's Gospel was that the people were there clinging to his every move, but for the wrong reasons. They were there for what they got out of it – in their case, being fed with bread and fish. We can sometimes get into the same 'craving rather than believing' mode if we are locked into receiving the spiritual or sacramental gifts for ourselves because they make us feel good. Jesus is not a restaurant where we indulge ourselves and eventually roll out home to bed; he is the Bread of Life, and supplies us with the food we need in order to live out his risen life among the people we are led to.

In Ephesians we are given an inspiring picture of such a life worked out in practical terms, enabled through our spiritual feeding to be built up in a co-ordinated body, displaying the characteristics of God's loving and humility.

Proper 14

Sunday between 7 and 13 August inclusive

Thought for the day

Just as bread is the visible form of life-giving
nourishment, so Jesus is the visible form of God's
life-giving love.

Reflection on the readings

2 Samuel 18:5-9, 15, 31-33 or 1 Kings 19:4-8
Psalm 130 or Psalm 34:1-8
Ephesians 4:25-5:2; John 6:35, 41-51

There are times when we have something important which
needs saying, but we know that it will be difficult to say
without being misunderstood. Jesus knew that what he was
saying would be hard for many to accept or understand, yet
he also knew it had to be said. The problem is that, unlike
young children, we all carry so much luggage and hurt
from our past that our listening is impaired. However good
our hearing, we block out and distort whatever we are not
wanting to receive, focus on the negatives and recycle
explanations as ammunition.

Much of praying and spiritual growth is to do with learning to listen, deliberately putting down our preconceptions,
pride and status, so that we are able to take in what God is
whispering into the humility of our unladen hearts. And,
sooner or later, that will always lead us to Jesus. Our Gospel
today homes in on a listening crisis, where the preparatory
work could all have been done, if those religious leaders had
been practising their Godly listening. Had that been the case,
they would have found themselves drawn, like the wise and
elderly Simeon, to see what God had been preparing them

for throughout their history: to recognise Jesus as the Bread from heaven – the visible expression of God's life and feeding.

In 1 Kings 19, Elijah is strengthened and refreshed on his journey to the mountain of God, and recognises that the baked loaf of bread and the jar of water are part of God's caring provision for him; even though he is emotionally drained and spiritually burnt out, he knows that it is God who is leading and feeding him. How wonderful it would have been if, on hearing those extraordinary words of Jesus – 'I am the bread that came down from heaven' – the religious leaders could have seen all the sense and truth of God's plan being worked out in front of their very eyes and in their hearing! But as it was, their habit of loaded listening prevented them from understanding.

The passage from Ephesians continues its practical advice to keep us open to God and able to listen with Godly understanding. There are marvellous hints like not letting the sun go down on our anger, and not letting the devil get even a toehold. There is much talk of shedding whatever prevents us from being built up in the life of Christ. The great news of hope which Jesus proclaims is that full life is possible as we recognise Jesus for who he is, and gladly receive his feeding.

Proper 15

Sunday between 14 and 20 August inclusive

Thought for the day

God's wisdom may appear foolishness without the God-given grace to understand.

Reflection on the readings

1 Kings 2:10-12; 3:3-14 or Proverbs 9:1-6
Psalm 111 or Psalm 34:9-14
Ephesians 5:15-20; John 6:51-58

Solomon asks for wisdom because he is acutely aware of his lack of experience and unreadiness for the task of reigning over God's people. Knowing his need makes him able to ask for it. We all need to recognise our ignorance in order to want to learn. In the passage from Proverbs the lady Wisdom calls out to those who recognise that they are simple, and want to increase their wisdom, which is in contrast to the lady Folly, who is encouraging people to drown out any higher calling and indulge their instincts and pleasure drives instead. Too late they will realise that her misleading call was to death, whereas Wisdom will lead her followers into a life of order and inner harmony.

In today's reading from Ephesians, too, we are advised to live wisely, making good use of every opportunity since the times are evil. The inference is that unless we are consciously walking positively in God's direction, we can so easily find ourselves sucked into the foolishness of living contrary to God's will for us. Wisdom is seen as living in inner peace and harmony with the God of our making.

If we are to get anywhere near such a state, we will need to walk expectantly and as disciples, rather than experts defending our position, and feeling offended every time we are tutored or instructed. In our Gospel for today, the religious leaders' status and learning was an enormous block to wisdom. They had too much to protect to risk walking in the nakedness of honesty.

We need to check any areas where we consider ourselves, or others consider us, experts or professionals, since these are precisely the areas where we shall find it hardest to place ourselves in the humility of discipleship.

It is hard for these learned religious teachers to understand his message, hung up as they are on precise detail instead of seeing the whole vision. They would hear Jesus' words not as a wonderful metaphor for God becoming one with his people through his Son, with all the wholesome nourishment and life-giving that the idea of bread contains; rather, they would hear it as a shocking blasphemy, with this wandering teacher aligning himself with the sacrificial Passover lamb and claiming to bring eternal freeing from sin. So they end up rejecting the fulfilment of the very idea they have studied and taught for years – that one day God will be 'with us' in person, and save us from our sin.

Proper 16

Thought for the day

'To whom else could we go?
You alone have the words of eternal life.'

Reflection on the readings

1 Kings 8:(1, 6, 10-11) 22-30, 41-43 or Joshua 24:1-2a, 14-18
Psalm 84 or Psalm 34:15-22
Ephesians 6:10-20; John 6:56-69

Most choices we make in life are fairly unimportant. It will probably make little difference whether we choose vanilla or raspberry ripple, ten o'clock or ten fifteen, chrysanthemums or asters. But the big important decision, which drives everything else we decide, is the direction we choose to face as we walk through life.

In our reading from Joshua, the significance of this commitment is made thoroughly clear to the people, since Joshua wants to be sure that everyone really knows what they are voting for, together with the potential cost as well as the benefits. Having laid out the facts, Joshua then gives the lead. He is not opting out of leadership and suggesting that either choice is as good as the other but offers one direction as choosing life, the other death, and takes his stand on the good choice as he declares, 'As for me and my household, we will serve the Lord.' The people whole-heartedly agree, basing their commitment on their actual experience of God's consistent loving care of them.

Similarly, in the reading from 1 Kings, we witness the consecration of the temple, in which King Solomon is again making a great national statement of commitment to the one true God whose name the house bears.

In a genuine but over-enthusiastic desire to allow free-dom and engender mutual respect, our own age tends now to distrust any absolutes, preferring to think of all truth as relative and a matter of individual choice. In such a climate it takes courage to profess our faith in Jesus Christ, and we may often find ourselves in the minority, or actively disputing widely accepted moral principles which run contrary to God's law of love.

So we hear with empathy today's Gospel reading, with many disciples walking away from Jesus now that he claims such a close relationship with the transcendent God. It is too much for them to come to terms with, and they conclude that Jesus has overstepped the mark. We too are faced with the same challenge. Either Jesus, as a good and gifted human being, has overreached his sanity, or he is speaking the truth. If the latter is so, he must indeed be the Holy One of God, with all that this implies for us in terms of commitment.

Proper 17

Thought for the day

We need to be careful never to replace the timeless commands of God with man-made traditions.

Reflection on the readings

Song of Solomon 2:8-13 or Deuteronomy 4:1-2, 6-9
Psalm 45:1-2, 6-9 or Psalm 15
James 1:17-27; Mark 7:1-8, 14-15, 21-23

In the reading from Deuteronomy the people are given reasons for valuing and upholding the Law of God as encapsulated in the ten commandments. One reason is that a community living according to such a Law will look very impressive to all the surrounding peoples, and point to the nation being full of wisdom and understanding. Another reason is that such a relationship with the living God will make all observers respect the obvious greatness of a nation so greatly blessed. However, this does depend on the people actually keeping the Law, and passing it down through the generations. That is crucial.

When we come to the passage from Mark, we find that a very human corruption of truth has been eating away at that wonderful ideal. We always find it so much easier to reduce vibrant truth to rigid, narrow rules. Insidiously the rules surrounding the truth take over in importance and are given permission to reign through the name of tradition, which is then reverenced, tragically at the expense of the original glorious, liberating vision. It is not just in Jewish religious teaching that this happens, but everywhere.

Jesus, with the clear insight of the Son of God, sees the terrible reality gap and its consequences. So corrupted has the perception of the Law become, that the very teachers are preventing the truth from catching hold of people's imagination, and in many cases the real meaning has been turned completely on its head. Jesus is not so much turning the world upside down by his teaching as turning it right side up again, the way God intended it to be.

Far from not keeping the Law, Jesus is reverencing it with his whole being, while the teachers have let go of the essence of God's truth and are left hanging on to scraggy handfuls of dry rules.

The reading from James is particularly helpful today since it comes from the Jewish tradition, with the fresh life of the Spirit breathed into it. Like the ancient prophets, the writer grounds God's truth in compassion and practical caring, coupled with a rigorous checking of personal purity so as to live in the wide freedom of God's law of love, which is altogether more demanding but also infinitely more fulfilling.

Proper 18

Sunday between 4 and 10 September inclusive

Thought for the day

Jesus comes fulfilling the hope of healing to wholeness;
he shows that mercy has triumphed over judgement.

Reflection on the readings

Proverbs 22:1-2, 8-9, 22-23 or Isaiah 35:4-7a
Psalm 125 or Psalm 146
James 2:1-10 (11-13) 14-17; Mark 7:24-37

In the Old Testament prophecies describing a healing
Messiah, we sense the huge waves of longing for the
whole nation to be restored and beautiful in God's sight,
in full and vigorous health morally, elementally, physically
and spiritually. Everything is pictured as bursting into
new life and vitality through the direct touch of God's
presence.

The reading from James picks up on the kind of healthy
attitudes which are free from prejudice and discrimination,
recognising that in the fullness of God our thinking is to be
reworked until it reflects God's character, and we celebrate
the triumph of mercy over judgement.

Today's Gospel shows Jesus acting all this out in person.
He doesn't advertise for custom, so as to force the events to
fit the promises of scripture; on the contrary, people drag
their loved ones to him and beg him to work God's healing
in them. Even as he sighed, 'Ephphatha!', longing in love
for the man's ears to be opened, it is as if he is longing for
the ears of the whole people of God to be opened so that
they may hear and understand.

Immediately before this healing, which exactly matches
with the expected touch of the Messiah, we are given

another healing which can sound initially offensive to our twenty-first-century ears. The woman asking for her daughter to be healed is both a Gentile and a foreigner, and Jesus' reaction to her seems to go against what we expect of the Saviour of the whole world. Surely this was a wonderful opportunity for him to show the Jewish community that God's healing is for everyone? Perhaps Jesus wanted to voice the traditional Jewish attitude on behalf of the people so they could see how God intended to overcome such barriers.

Certainly Jesus' first priority was obedience to the Father. Since he knew that his mission was to bring the good news to the Jewish people, he was hesitant about the timing of this outreach, just as he had said to his mother at Cana, 'My hour has not yet come.' Always he was communing with the Father, keeping exactly in step with him, however that might look from the outside. The wonderful thing is that God uses this woman to reassure his Son. As she gives him the picture of crumbs dropping as the children eat, Jesus sees how much in line this overflow of blessing is with God's will, and gladly restores her daughter to health.

Proper 19

Thought for the day

Loving obedience to God is shown by Jesus
to be a quality rich in courage and wisdom,
a quality to be highly respected.

Reflection on the readings

Proverbs 1:20-33 or Isaiah 50:4-9a
Psalm 19 or Wisdom of Solomon 7:26-8:1 or Psalm 116:1-9
James 3:1-12; Mark 8:27-38

Obedience is currently rather a despised quality, and certainly not one which most people would strive to develop. Rather the opposite, since it has connotations for us of being somewhat immature and not yet our own, independent person if we claim to place any store by it. Not surprisingly, children pick this up in adults and copy it. Children learn discipline and self-control from disciplined, self-controlled adults, who value obedience themselves.

The passage from Proverbs speaks of wisdom being the willingness to listen to advice and take it, and to accept rebuke so as to learn. That is all part of obedience, the getting into a position where we can hear and accept a superior's teaching. Those who refuse the offer are considered simple and foolish, in terms of eternity.

As the prophet in the book of Isaiah speaks of the figure of the Servant in complete loving obedience to God, his hearers would understand that here is someone of perfect wisdom and harmony with God, humble and courageous enough to do what is required as Saviour, whatever the personal cost. Though the people might well rebel in full-blooded human style, they recognised the importance and good sense of obedience.

In the letter of James the early Church is roundly chastised by the exasperated elder who has presumably come across yet another disaster caused by ill-disciplined tongues! And he's right – that small organ is capable of so much harm, and we'd do well to take James' passionate outburst to heart, not least in the conversations immediately following our worship each week. Again, it's our dislike of living obediently. If only God would turn his back for a minute while we say or do what we know he'd tell us not to!

But our example is Jesus, and today we meet him at the point when his disciples are beginning to grasp who he is, so he starts to explain what this will involve. It's too much for his friends. If Jesus isn't going to protest, then they will. Satan is quite happy to use well-meant persuasion to tempt us away from obedience. Thankfully Jesus stands firm, and lays out the obedience needed for all potential followers. Are we prepared to take him up on it?

Proper 20

Thought for the day

The truly great in God's eyes are those who are
prepared to be last of all and servant of all.

Reflection on the readings

Proverbs 31:10-31 or Wisdom of Solomon 1:16-2:1, 12-22
or Jeremiah 11:18-20; Psalm 1 or Psalm 54
James 3:13-4:3, 7-8a; Mark 9:30-37

Plato reckoned that the only people suitable for leadership
and positions of power were those who would never want to
do it. The corrupting influence of power is clear for all to see,
and we can all think of people in positions of greatness who
are there through their ambition rather than their suitability
for the office! In today's candid Gospel the disciples are not
spared the gaze of the world at their petty arguing about
which of them is most important, carrying most status. As we
recall our own (probably private) conversations about what
people think of us, we can humble ourselves with them as
we listen to Jesus' teaching.

The kind of values we usually set store by are upended
by Jesus' criteria for greatness. Being the last of all and the
servant of all is, for a start, likely to go unnoticed and
unappreciated most of the time. But we usually would
expect praise and acknowledgement for humble service,
and grumble if it wasn't forthcoming. Jesus is talking
about enjoying working for others without recognition;
keeping such service secret as far as possible.

The little child is a dramatic visual aid of the vulnerable
and those of lowest status, without rights or wealth or

power. And Jesus is suggesting that we consider ourselves servants with fewer rights than these little ones. We are to gather up all our ambitions about wealth, power and status, which are bound to affect our attitudes to others, and scatter them on the wind, leaving us free and unburdened, so that we can simply serve others in humility and love. We have the shining example of such a life in Jesus himself.

All the battles and strife which James talks about stem from this drive to be considered best, or to be better than other people. Often we ground this drive in our desire to possess money, things, qualifications, people, or any kind of trophy. Sadly, none of it impresses God, and none of it helps us fulfil our true selves, even though Satan persuades us that it will give us what we crave. As James suggests, we need to stand up to Satan and then we will find he slinks away, and we are already totally valued, so there was no need to strive after any of those things. Loving and obedient service, in simple humility, is what gladdens the heart of God, who already loves us completely.

Proper 21

Thought for the day

Don't let your body lead you into sin and risk
exchanging eternal life for eternal punishment.

Reflection on the readings

Esther 7:1-6, 9-10; 9:20-22 or Numbers 11:4-6, 10-16, 24-29
Psalm 124 or Psalm 19:7-14
James 5:13-20; Mark 9:38-50

Nobody talks much about hell. We have moved away from the graphic fire and brimstone images of the medieval artists, and tend to pass over Jesus' teaching about it. But sometimes we have to address it, and today is one of those days.

Jesus had a lot of hard sayings for his disciples to swallow. They needed to understand and accept, for instance, that God doesn't rigidly limit his Spirit to work within the Church. Joshua had been just as offended by the seventy elders all prophesying, and Moses had to remind him that as far as he was concerned he'd be happy for the whole community to be filled with the Spirit of God. God doesn't limit his power to those of specific groups. We, too, need have no problem with Christian work being done by those outside the Church.

And then there is the hard but clear teaching on the importance of self-control. Jesus is not pretending temptation is easy to cope with. He knew from personal experience that it was agonisingly difficult. It is always a struggle to resist temptation, and fighting it can feel as drastic as chopping off hands or feet, or plucking out eyes. Even hearts, if they are causing us to sin and distracting us from God. It is because we don't take temptation seriously enough that we so often fall into sin. Jesus, in his agony in the garden, as he watched and prayed desperately to resist the temptation to opt out of the work of salvation, urges Peter and the others to do the same, so that they will not fall when the onslaught of temptation engulfs them, but they slept instead.

The reason for Jesus' urgent concern for us is that sin has eternal terrible consequences that we can barely imagine. It is forfeiting eternal life we are talking about, and some kind of eternal punishment which certainly fills Jesus with horror to think of. If he was taking it that seriously, then surely we would be wise to do the same. We are called to be preservatives – like salt – working at preserving souls for a glorious eternal life which is God's will for us all. We can't do that if we are allowing our own bodies and attitudes to lead us deep into sin. Neither can we kid ourselves we are preservatives unless we are actively committed to helping others towards the kingdom.

Proper 22
Sunday between 2 and 8 October inclusive

Thought for the day

Human beings are made responsible for the care of creation but are subject to God in all aspects of their lives.

Reflection on the readings

Job 1:1; 2:1-10 or Genesis 2:18-24; Psalm 26 or Psalm 8
Hebrews 1:1-4; 2:5-12; Mark 10:2-16

In the reading from Job we are shown a man who recognises and accepts his place under God, and who will not be persuaded to curse his creator on account of his sufferings. To Job they, as well as the joys of life, are part of the deal and we have no right to expect all sunshine.

In the Genesis reading we look at the more ancient and primitive of the creation stories, with Adam being taken around the freshly made world, naming the animals and thus being established as responsible for the care of creation. No animal being suitable as a helpmate, woman is created from Adam, though for this 'birthing' Adam is anaesthetised and spared the pain! (Floating ribs would have become separated in skeletons seen around at the time of writing, possibly giving rise to the idea of woman being created from a spare rib.)

The deep truth of the story lies in God creating people who are given responsibility while remaining subject to God, their creator. The 'God with man and woman' teamwork is established right at the start of history. It is just as fresh and definite now, and we must not shirk that responsibility, under God, to care for the universe we inhabit. We are not called to dominate it and squeeze it dry for our own short-sighted indulgence, but to be careful stewards in every generation.

That careful stewardship extends to our own lives as well, and all our relationships, particularly marriage. Choosing life partners is a serious matter for God and us to consider carefully together, and the upholding of marriage is the responsibility of the whole community. Jesus takes his disciples back to this basic established pattern when he reinforces the importance of lifelong faithfulness in marriage. We cannot tear these verses out of the Gospel simply because they are at variance with society's norms. Jesus is describing God's good intention for those called to marriage to live in the security and comfort of lifelong partnership under his banner of love.

Of course there will be cases where, due to our hardness of heart, our wrong choices or through other pressures, the ideal falters and relationships break down irreparably. Those are occasions of deep sadness for the whole community, for a recognition of our brokenness, for repentance and forgiveness. They do not alter the wonderful provision God has made for us.

Proper 23

Sunday between 9 and 15 October inclusive

Thought for the day

The word of God is living and active, piercing right to the
heart; only with God is it possible to be saved.

Reflection on the readings

Job 23:1-9, 16-17 or Amos 5:6-7, 10-15
Psalm 22:1-15 or Psalm 90:12-17
Hebrews 4:12-16; Mark 10:17-31

The prophet Amos urges his hearers to seek the Lord and
live, implying that unless they actively seek God and his
goodness, truth and justice, they will find themselves
unable to inherit God's blessings in their lives or their
nation. The alternative Old Testament reading from Job
shows us in contrast a God-fearing, upright man who is
steadfastly seeking God with all his heart, even though he
feels surrounded by thick darkness and unable to find him.
Even in the darkness and silence, Job continues to seek,
trusting that God knows where he is and will eventually
reveal himself.

Seeking God is a quest that alters our whole outlook on
life. It isn't a casual hobby, or a weekend interest. While we
actively seek God, we will be listening and looking atten-
tively, and this will move us to question our own motives
for doing things, and the way we behave. We cannot be
seeking God, for instance, if we are trampling on all that is
right and good, despising those who tell the truth and
crushing the poor. If we are honest and serious in our search,
the very seeking will begin to change us, by changing our
hearts.

The writer of Hebrews has obviously seen and experienced this process, and likens the power of the word of God to a sharp sword – or perhaps for us the image of a surgeon's scalpel – with its precise, clean cut, enabling the healing work to be done. Once the thoughts and attitudes of our hearts are being transformed, through God's power, then the impossible business of conquering sin becomes a distinct possibility; hope is in sight for us at last!

The young man in today's Gospel is keen. He comes running up to Jesus, wanting to know how he can inherit eternal life. Typically, Jesus doesn't answer directly, but picks up on the young man's thinking, as shown in calling Jesus 'good'. His seeking has already led him to recognise goodness in this preacher, and Jesus helps him further along, to look at what God's ideas of goodness are, and where that challenges the young man's life. When he moves away frowning, it isn't that he disagrees with Jesus, but that he has just realised he is right.

Like the young man, we who seek will find Jesus challenging us, and then we have to choose whether to go on with the search, or press cancel.

Proper 24

Thought for the day

Even the Son of Man himself came not to be served but to serve, and to give his life as a ransom for many.

Reflection on the readings

Job 38:1-7 (34-41) or Isaiah 53:4-12
Psalm 104:1-9, 24, 35c or Psalm 91:9-16
Hebrews 5:1-10; Mark 10:35-45

Job has continued to seek God through the bleakness and silence, and now it is as if God suddenly throws open the door so wide that Job almost falls over. With the joy of an answer comes the humbling question of what right any of us have to expect to understand, or to challenge the great Creator of the universe, the One who is the ground of our being.

In the Isaiah reading we have one of the extraordinary prophecies about God's suffering servant, which we, in the light of the Gospels, see as so perceptive in grasping the inevitable suffering of God's Saviour, Jesus. The writer of Hebrews helps us to understand it. Although the Messiah figure for many was seen as a national leader who would establish his reign and drive out oppressors, the more spiritual Messianic dream was that he would be a priestly king, mystically anointed with the power of Yahweh himself, taking on the suffering of the people with God's blessing, so that they may be saved.

Humans find it so hard to break away from the power and hierarchy models of thinking. Even though James and John have spent two or three years living and working with

Jesus, have gone out on mission preaching the kingdom and experiencing many miracles, being dragged off to meals with rich and poor, socially elite and social outcasts alike, they are still thinking in worldly terms of greatness and status.

I suspect they might, at the time, have protested at that, and believed they were asking to sit at Jesus' right and left for noble reasons, like feeling themselves so close to their master, and wanting that to continue for ever. Who knows. Jesus is wonderfully forgiving of their inane suggestion, so alien to all he is. We can imagine him shaking his head helplessly as he says, 'You don't know what you're asking!' James and John are like so many of us, arrogant in our ignorant enthusiasm.

Today's message is really to do with that humble obedience which comes through suffering and persevering when the going is tough, and eventually makes us wise enough to listen with our hearts to what is really important.

Proper 25

Thought for the day

In Jesus, God gathers his scattered people
and opens their eyes to see.

Reflection on the readings

Job 42:1-6, 10-17 or Jeremiah 31:7-9
Psalm 34:1-8, 19-22 or Psalm 126
Hebrews 7:23-28; Mark 10:46-52

In the reading from Job, the vision of God's tender and comprehensive care of all creation, and his love in bringing it all to being, results in Job recognising God's true greatness at a deeper level. In new reverence and humility he bows before God, who gathers him up and lavishes his blessings on this honest and suffering man.

In the passage from Jeremiah, the prophet longs for the people to find again a close, personal relationship with the living God. No more empty, formalised religious practice, but a real reverence and tender returning to the Lord who loves them. He describes it as if it is happening, with streams of scattered people, all with their needs and frailty, being drawn from the ends of the earth, weeping and praying as they realise who they are, and whose they are.

The writer of Hebrews reinforces this joy of finding in Jesus the Saviour who meets our needs, providing for us what we by ourselves cannot achieve. Only Jesus, as the go-between, priestly figure of all time, is holy, blameless, pure, and set apart from sinners, yet willingly taking their part.

The Gospel reading catapults us into the kingdom longed for by the prophets. Here, in the dusty main street on the way out of Jericho town, we find the promised Christ going about his healing business of giving sight to the blind. Bartimaeus is anxious not to miss out on this opportunity, and it is his faith, Jesus tells him, which heals his sight. In the reality of this beggar, happy and freed from blindness, choosing to follow Jesus, we glimpse the wider vision of the whole of the world returning, with tears of joy running down their faces, to the God who never gives up on them and longs to gather them to himself.

All Saints' Day

Thought for the day

Great is the rejoicing in heaven among the saints of God
as they worship their Lord in glory.

Reflection on the readings

Wisdom 3:1-9 or Isaiah 25:6-9; Psalm 24:1-6
Revelation 21:1-6a; John 11:32-44

When we have the handed-down stories of the saints, and
the stained-glass pictures of them with sun streaming
through and bathing us in coloured light as we kneel, praying, it is perhaps inevitable that we think of the saints as a
different breed from ourselves. With all the noble things they
did and persevered at, it's somehow hard to imagine them
doing ordinary things like getting irritated by the length of
queue at the checkout, or shouting at the children. We rather
imagine them unruffled by the things which give most of us
grey hairs, sailing through their deep, spiritual sufferings,
helped by some saintly gene we haven't inherited.

Perhaps the most important thing we celebrate today is
that, however we have since reworked their lives, and however beautiful their monuments, saints begin as ordinary as
the rest of us, and it is just as possible for all of us to be
saintly as it was for them and everyone else in their class at
school. But would we want to be? Even the word 'saintly'
has unfortunate connotations for some, suggesting an insuf-
ferable 'goody goody' character and a loss of contact with
reality to be avoided at all costs.

Wrong again. Real saints have their feet fixed firmly in
the real world, loving and appreciating it. They are people

taking the 'Love God; love one another' code seriously, and you can't do that from an ethereal distance. Loving means getting involved, getting hurt, seeing the funny side (sometimes), learning from your embarrassing mistakes and all your experiences. These are real, ordinary people with their individual ways and habits, and lots of times in their lives when they had no idea what the next step should be.

The point is that they became saints through living ordinary lives, closely in God's company. The refining of lives takes place through living, and no one can side-step that requirement. As Jesus said, if we try to protect and shield our life we end up not keeping it safe but losing it. It is those who daily give it joyfully away who end up gaining the heavenly life which lasts for ever.

Fourth Sunday before Advent

Sunday between 30 October and 5 November inclusive*

* For use if the Feast of All Saints was celebrated on
1 November and alternative propers are needed

Thought for the day

To love the living God with heart, soul and strength,
and to love our neighbour as ourselves means
far more than any sacrificial offerings.

Reflection on the readings

Deuteronomy 6:1-9; Psalm 119:1-8
Hebrews 9:11-14; Mark 12:28-34

We might wonder why a scribe, highly educated in the
law, should ask Jesus the seemingly obvious question:
'Which is the first among all the commandments?' Surely
he knows that? But, as in any discipline, the simplest
sounding questions are often the most complex to experts,
and the Jewish academics spent much time puzzling over
the huge number of accumulated laws, so it had become
hard to see the wood for the trees. Genuinely this scribe is
wanting to search out right priorities – or indeed to establish whether any prioritising would be insulting to God.

Jesus' answer, coming after the discussions with those out
to trick and test him, responds to this scribe's honest searching with perhaps the most powerful statement of faith ever
uttered. Here is the Son of the living God, standing among
his own people, in direct line from the patriarchs, prophets
and King David, proclaiming the Shema: 'Hear, O Israel!
The Lord our God is the one Lord!' To all Jewish people,
this expression of faith is profoundly precious, a kind of

'passport into paradise' for every child of Abraham, spoken three times every day by every believer. What must it have sounded like in this context, spoken by this voice? I would love to have been there!

All the love, all the obedience, all the authority, inspired the scribe to recognise, with fresh understanding, the wonder of those words, and the following summary of the law. We can hear in his excited response that he has seen the fresh colours of God's law again, as if the accumulated varnish from generations has been cleaned away, and the original beauty and brightness is startlingly visible.

Right back in the Deuteronomy reading, the significance and importance of this statement and law was urged upon the people. They were to wear it, tie it on gates and attach it to doorposts, passing it on to their children and grand-children so as to ensure its continued obedience, and the psalmists meditated on the joy and blessing resulting from keeping God at the heart of our lives.

The writer of Hebrews, speaking to a Jewish audience, explores the work of Jesus in terms of Jewish sacrifices, right at the heart of their worship of the one true God. Time and again the priests needed to offer sacrifices on behalf of the people; in Jesus, both high priest and sacrificial victim, the total sacrifice is accomplished once and for all.

Third Sunday before Advent

Sunday between 6 and 12 November inclusive

Thought for the day

When we are called we need to respond with obedience
so that many may be brought to repentance.

Reflection on the readings

Jonah 3:1-5, 10; Psalm 62:5-12
Hebrews 9:24-28; Mark 1:14-20

It's 'Take two' as far as Jonah is concerned, following the first
calling which had resulted in his marching smartly away in
the opposite direction, with fairly drastic consequences. Typically, God's call hasn't changed when he eventually gets
Jonah's attention again; he just quietly repeats into Jonah's
heart what Jonah knows is the right thing to do. And this
time he obeys God's calling, with the result that the people of
Nineveh come to a dramatic, collective repentance, and are
saved from destruction.

The psalmist urges us to put our trust in God, who is rock-
like in his firm faithfulness and protection. In comparison,
all else is considered air-headed rubbish, bound to dis-
appoint and let us down.

The passage from Hebrews continues to show us how
Jesus the Christ draws to completion and fulfilment all the
sacrificial history of God's people. The tent of the Holy of
Holies was set apart from the camps in the desert, and it was
a sacred, holy occasion when Moses entered the tent. The
writer sees Jesus' entry into heaven as the real fulfilment of
what that image of the tent was saying. He looks forward to
the second coming which will not be dealing with sin, since
that is now accomplished, but rather the bringing-in of
promised salvation.

The Gospel swings us back to Jesus first striding out into ministry, announcing the coming kingdom of God and urging repentance and belief in the good news. No sooner has he started to alert people, than he begins to gather workers for the harvest, calling fishermen from casting and mending their nets to reaching people and mending them through God's love. Their obedience to his call is vital for the saving of many.

Second Sunday before Advent

Sunday between 13 and 19 November inclusive

Thought for the day

We are to be on our guard; great anguish will accompany the last days, but all that is good and loving, wise and true will be saved and celebrated for ever.

Reflection on the readings

Daniel 12:1-3; Psalm 16
Hebrews 10:11-14 (15-18) 19-25; Mark 13:1-8

As the darkness crowds further into each day for those of us in the northern hemisphere, we have a powerful reminder of the gathering evil which it is foretold will accompany the heralding in of the last days. Jesus smelt it with the nose of a prophet, and although no exact dates can be given, he is very concerned for his disciples to understand the importance for them and us to be on our guard. We do indeed need to take great care as we walk and drive through our time on earth. All around us are subtle and powerful temptations to steer us off course, and distract us from our calling.

As we begin to experience the effects of our shrinking world, and recognise our interdependence, we are aware of the opportunities provided for mutual damage and instability as well as positive partnership. Large-scale damage of evil is increasingly possible and harder to prevent.

All is not gloom and doom, however. For those already living the risen life, the fear of annihilation is actually irrelevant, and the last day should fill us with excitement and hope, rather than terror, since at that time of accomplishment, all goodness, love, wisdom and truth will be revealed for what it is, shining and beautiful, and lasting for ever.

The psalmist describes his spiritual inheritance as if he is walking around the pleasant farmland which he knows will become his own as soon as he comes of age. He is pleased with the patch God has chosen for him and enjoys it in the present as well as for the future. Perhaps that gives us a model to work with.

We know and are thrilled that Jesus Christ has secured salvation for us, and our hope for that last day is not in our own ragged and scarred lives, but in the victory of the cross. The reason for being on our guard in these last days is not that the promise of salvation may suddenly be snatched away from us, but that in all the evil we may choose to throw away our hope of salvation. If we stay faithful through all the troubles which there are bound to be, we have nothing to fear at all, but rather a celebration to look forward to.

Christic the King

Thought for the day

Jesus Christ is the everlasting King whose kingdom
is not of this world, but grows in the hearts of
his people and lasts for ever.

Reflection on the readings

Daniel 7:9-10, 13-14; Psalm 93
Revelation 1:4b-8; John 18:33-37

It is always difficult to describe heavenly things in terms of
our human experience, but Daniel tries to give a faithful
account of his vision of the one he calls the Ancient of Days,
sensing the everness of his wisdom and power, his piercing
integrity and all-knowing perception. Images of rivers of
fire, thrones and vast crowds worshipping help to give us
some idea of God's glory as the source and sustainer of all.
Daniel witnesses the moment of one like a son of man entering heaven and receiving the authority and dominion
which are his for ever.

We who have met Jesus in the Gospels, and heard him
refer often to himself as 'Son of Man', recognise the one
who enters heaven as the Lord and Saviour who loved us
enough to die for us. The Gospel for today refers us to Jesus'
conversation with Pilate, just before his crucifixion. Jesus
tells the Roman governor, who represents the worldly
power and authority of the whole Roman Empire, that his
kingdom is not of this world. He is not therefore a threat to
the authorities in terms of violent uprising and revolt. The
kingdom of God is a lot more powerful, far-reaching and
long-lasting than any empire!

In the reading from Revelation we are back in the world of vision and prophecy, written for those who had witnessed the crucifixion and resurrection of Christ, the outpouring of God's Spirit in tongues of flame, and the business of living as followers of Christ in an often hostile world. There will come a time when Christ the everlasting King will appear in all his glory, and every eye shall see him.

The Church's year has come full circle. We began last Advent by preparing ourselves for the coming of Jesus, both at his birth into our world and at the second coming. We have walked with Jesus through his life and ministry, led mainly this year by Mark's dynamic Gospel account. We have watched Jesus and listened to him, sorrowed and rejoiced with him. We have seen the gradual understanding of the disciples and their transformation through the gift of the Holy Spirit. And now, as we celebrate Jesus, King of all ages and nations, born for this, living and dying and rising for this, we proclaim the basic Christian belief which will enable us to press forward into our Advent preparations: Jesus Christ is Lord!